100 Cassettes

Dennis Callaci

Pelekinesis

100 Cassettes by Dennis Callaci

ISBN: 978-1-949790-19-1

eISBN: 978-1-949790-20-7

Library of Congress Control Number: 2019945714

Copyright © 2020 Dennis Callaci

Artwork by Dennis Callaci

Layout and book design by Mark Givens

First Pelekinesis Printing 2020

For information:

Pelekinesis, 112 Harvard Ave #65, Claremont, CA 91711 USA

www.pelekinesis.com

100 Cassettes

DENNIS CALLACI

SHRIMPER
PO BOX 1837
UPLAND, CA 91785

For the home recorders,
home tapers,
and
home team

CONTENTS

INTRODUCTION
BY JONATHAN LETHEM

I HAVE A PERSISTENT AND EMBARRASSING morbid self-aggrandizing fantasy about the songs I will force a large convocation of my loved ones to listen to at my funeral. A last DJ set for a captive audience, whom I foolishly envision, despite wishing for myself a slow decline into a mellow elderlyhood including several books written in my, ahem "late style," as being the assemblage of younger selves I want my family and friends to remain forever. Not bloody likely. So, either old exhausted people who can't dance and maybe can't hear the full sonic range and are just wishing I wouldn't torture them with my from-the-grave set list, or else this is a fantasy about dying—well, not young, too late for that, but soon. Middle-aged. I said embarrassing and morbid and self-aggrandizing, right? Some days it's nearly all Kinks' songs ("This Time Tomorrow," "Big Sky," "Days," etc.) Most every time there's an Al Green or Marvin Gaye track ("Chariots of Fire?" "Time?"). A peculiar late-era Joni Mitchell song that always cracks the memory-vault code for me, "Coming In From the Cold." Usually "I Love This Life" by Blue Nile, which no one really likes but me, and for which Dennis Callaci has specifically mocked me in the aisles of Rhino Records—but he also located for me a copy of a CD signed by all four members of Blue Nile, a thing I'll treasure forever and get framed as soon as I can locate it again where it is lurking in my storage area.

Why, when all I had to do here was function as Dennis's opening act, play a little fast-loud-rules and decline the temptation to take the mild cheers as incitement to an encore lest I get booed off stage—why, in this simple task, have I come on strong with death rites? Friends, think of this overture as a warning sticker, as on a chemistry set: emotionally volatile contents herein. The book in your hands is an autumn almanac, a labyrinthine feels-machine, one all the more disarming for coming on as alternate-reality caprice—hey, these records don't exist, so how can they possibly break your heart? Sure, maybe us fading humans will pause to wallow over the recentest landmine losses (we got your Cohen and Petty and Prince right here), but shouldn't those just be the bittersweet morsels in the fannish cookie? But no. It's a cumulative thing, which is to say, a real book. It kicked my ass again and again and increasingly, until somewhere at the intersection of Chris Bell and David Ruffin I understood that this book wasn't in my hands, but the reverse. Many of these "cassettes" made me cry, though I'm mostly not going to tell you which ones; they might surprise you, as they surprised me. I'm a soft touch, sure, but when I'm shedding tears about Biz Markie you can be sure that the dancing about architecture has reached unusual heights—it might even have turned out to be architecture about dancing. Callaci conjures a mix of fiction and trivia and memoir and secret code, and when I say "I wish I'd written it myself" I mean that I wish I thought I could have, or even knew exactly how it works. Just because I'm introducing it doesn't mean I've figured this out. "How many strays is one home expected to take in?"—that's one line that haunts the whole mansion here, a beauty, and the answer to the question appears to be: every single one that appears at your door, until the day you go stray yourself, and someone else has to take up the job. Maybe I'll get someone to read *100 Cassettes* aloud at my funeral – that'll show 'em.

100 Cassettes

GO-BETWEENS

THE YEAR BEFORE my mother-in-law passed away and my father-in-law fell ill, I had switched gears. Catherine and I would take in long weekend mornings with coffee and bedding instead of working in the yard or the kitchen or the kitchen table with bills. On weeknights, I would write and work on songs at a pace that I hadn't sped at since my 20's. My body knew something that my mind didn't as I spent six months piecing together a thirty minute song for release. What is before you is not a song, so I feel that I can reveal the seams and bone. I would listen to music two, three, four nights a week. DJing to myself, maybe Catherine if she was working on the checkbook, Henry, our youngest, who surely heard the racket crawling down the hallway and into his room. One night I made a scrawl of Robert Forster of The Go-Betweens in one of my lyric books, Catherine wandered into the room I was in, and I imagine what I looked like had my Ma caught me masturbating thirty five years previously. What are you doing? I dunno. Cuz I didn't know. I know now. I was preparing. I was lining up all of my secular saints so that they would float me over the future before us that I couldn't then see. I pulled out some legal sized paper from the hall closet and cropped twenty or so pages to the size of cassette J-cards on the paper cutter that I had used to cut thousands upon thousands of covers for cassettes. I started drawing as I was listening, imagining forgotten releases by artists that I held as near to my heart as I could get them along with asterisked bands that I fleetingly had affairs with. No intention of anything, nothing.

These drawings are all fantasy, a common fantasy. You have certainly read books about aborted films, could have been records, fake correspondence, or make believe projects by a writer's favorite artist. These drawings started as something to do while I listened to records one night, no real plan. Just a fantasy, a stupid one at best built on sharpies, water colors, pencils, ball points & typing paper.

Caveat emptor 1: After I had 100 covers done, I put an end to it. There was nothing to add that wouldn't seem redundant, or ridiculous (truth be told about 10 of the drawings went to the trash bin and I would say this book would be all the stronger if another 25 met that same fate). I tried to make up for the weaker ideas or cover illustrations by bringing some levity or weight to the script herein. If this is your kind of thing, well, you get the table scraps and all of the outtakes in one fell swoop.[1]

Caveat emptor 2: The dA Center for the Arts was kind enough to glass case the completed cassettes for an installation at the beginning of 2018. In the spring of that same year, I started writing pieces to accompany each cassette. It wasn't until I got ankle deep in writing that the writing revealed to me that most of what I was penning was non-fiction. Early entries were easy, a history of how an artist touched me or maybe here and there, hadn't. The chalk on gravestone started turning up biographies. A song about a friend, a record that called back my sister, an artist whose music buoyed me through rockier health or marital troubles (if you plan to be married for twenty five years or more to the same person, there are rocky rivers), a number of the entries became personal, autobiographical.

What peppers this book and brought it all out of me was a record store. I was raised in record stores and I work in a couple of them during the week. I have no formal training to do anything. I took three years of Latin at Montclair High School but most of it is now lost on me. Cavity emperor.

Caveat emptor 3: You can do whatever you want in this life, no one is paying any attention to you. Go on ahead, approach

---

1   http://www.pelekinesis.com/catalog/dennis_callaci-100_cassettes-artwork.html

the stage, push to the front, put on a guitar, and scream into the mic. Everything is always recording, but no one is ever playing back the results. Quick, slip in, between the shadows, now, while you can't be seen. No one is watching, no one is paying attention to you. They are scripting. "What will I say next?" "What shall I next not do?" I'd rather, beside you, mistakenly, make a couple of wrong moves to get right. Get right with the lord the philanderer sang, do right the gospel choir underlined, the unexamined life is the only one without missteps and outtakes.

Here is everything; the typos, the awkward red pen highlights, a preordained script of images I was tethered to as I went about writing a hundred chapters. Don't worry; no one is aware of anything the two of us are doing right now. They are looking at their phones and other imaginary windows longingly. Hurry, let's get out past the bluffs and into the weeds where we can't be seen.

The news drips down here with kerosene
the three of us are careful to separate the flammable from the
    unremarkable
wood chip
linoleum cut
and even easier stuff
was complex in your hand
six feet dead asleep
poplars
falling leaves
an unsuccessful shake of an I Ching
black Irish poetry
the things 22-year-olds dress as to define
a 22-year-old state of mind

it is us and the dust
rustling around our bed
soon enough
indistinguishable

25 years back a frameless apartment in Brisbane
the 3 of you obscured by dirty french doors
3000 miles away in a locker room at a packing plant
no watch
I timed my paycheck by passing trains
2 every hour
22 and I'm home
2 every hour
22 and I'm home
getting up to 20
and I feel it in my bones
getting up to 20 and I feel it in my bones

the other day I was in a super real market
wrote the wrong date on my check hoping that the clerk would say
wrote the wrong date on my check hoping that the clerk would say
and the attendant from the cinema behind me she'd have to agree
those rumors never came to pass
that stranger he's not dead
that stranger,
he's not dead
and you'd awake from some low rent 40 thread count sheet bed
and begin again
I feel it in my bones

TAMMY WYNETTE
SKULLS AND HEARTS

HER OLDER SISTER lived in Thousand Oaks, another in Whittier. When the three of us were younger, we bounced between those two cities on the weekends. Their husbands were absent men: one a fighter of fires, the other an AC repairman. Both of them worked incredibly hard, providing for their families. Building towards something; cabins in the sky for one, cabins in the deep woods later in life for the other. There were arguments in my household from the age of two to five. I recall the dog leash being tethered to my father's leg while he and my mom argued for what seemed like hours over the kitchen table. The argument was so intense that even the endlessly complicated act for a two and six-year-old, with their clumsy little cinnamon taste-T picked toothpick fingers, wrapping that leash for hours around my father's leg, unnoticed, unfelt, unseen by him, was the first miracle that I recall witnessing even as it fell to the ground. He didn't stay. He couldn't stay. It could have been days later, or it could have been a number of months, there is no longer even a single memory of any other days in between. Us piling into Mom's car, just her and three kids, her careful so as to not hit that dwarf shrub at the northernmost end of the lawn, the one we would come back to years later and hide our action figures in. The one that just before we moved in my mid-teens, came up so easily with a shovel that I recall standing dumbfounded as the translucent roots upside downed the driveway.

There was square dancing at the community center in Thousand Oaks. May as well have been a head of state dinner, even then, I knew I was not only out of my water but out of my league.

These complicated algorithms, equations that reflecting back on now, well, they must have served as a respite for the Catholics, Protestants, Mormons, non-denominational entities of some kind who gathered together, submitted to that there summer day, and agreed upon a socially acceptable way of physically touching one another. The lights were on, and there were plenty of people around. They could fool themselves that nothing untoward could possibly be happening. Now, well past middle age, having seen the most disturbing and unbelievable of things in large crowds, in good company, I don't feel that sense of security. Not alone, not in crowds. These other worlds we visit, while they might be a kick to take in briefly, they are all the same in that they offer no true escape; just the fleeting and the momentary. I imagine now how dead-ended that street then must have felt for you, rudderless and simultaneously tied down by three children. You were no longer visiting. You couldn't then support even just yourself in an attempt to make a living. Here you were, living in a city of default, with sidewalks instead of lemon groves and unpaved, unincorporated neighboring hamlets.

Little Leagues, cub scouts, drill teams—some sense of normalcy for lonely children whose parents floated into the ether on vodka tonics and Kent cigarette rough morning Pall Mall landings. Who worked as civil servants tirelessly, then, come evening, wontedly waiting for only sleep. Used car nightclubs, checker board apartment swimming pool lifestyles, parents without partners exchanging vagaries at the local stop n' shop, folding hand-me-arounds at laundromats whose embraces were graffittied in lower case Bic "fucks" - the knowing nod, the embarrassed so long. So, so long, that it was no longer embarrassing. It was just day-to-day. There were songs then, on the AM band that spoke to them and their plights. "You Better Sit Down Kids," "Rainy Days And Mondays," "D-I-V-O-R-C-E," "Delta Dawn," "Caught In a Trap" - it was a God Damned musical pandemic. The most hushed and black beautied of orchestral flourishes masking the isolated rage of unanswered happy endings. Everyone was hurting, no one was in love. It was 1971, then 1973 bleeding into '75, no George McGovern coming to rescue nobody. There would be disco to pull our souls out of Vietnam as an afterword, and there would be second marriages that were built on lesser hopes then, in the late '70s. In our tiny malformed minds, as children of that decade, it was as though our hearts had been pulled from some Thailand-made Toys R Us piggy bank, fully-formed, with nothing on the inside. Go on, something in me said, take yer toy Plasticine hammer and break into the rib cage of the thing, the pink clay shattering, revealing in the guts nothing of surprise. Nickels and dimes, aluminum foil, Hershey kissed former flags, plastic game piece slugs, nothing worth much of anything. It would be decades later before I would be able to piece it all together, how kept and captive you must have felt. You, a fallen acorn passed around in some foreign beings teeth. I can hear your voice now, whispering "I need to get out of here, out of here with my kids in one piece."

BH FAIRCHILD
READS SELECTIONS FROM
THE ELECTRIC LATHE

H E WAS BORN ON THE PLAINS, but it was the written word, the printing press, literature, and poetry that became his domain. Economical poems about your friends and neighbors (well, if you have ever lived in lower- to middle-class neighborhoods) both in the everyday and in the ether, dropping their bodies to the kitchen tile and floating up and away. His book *Early Occult Memory Systems Of The Lower Midwest* is perhaps the best title for a book of poetry that has ever been put forth. Sorry Milton, apologies Dante. Is it proper to call this autobiographical book a set of poems? The poems themselves break from any A/B/A/B or A/B/C/B conventions.

Through a powder blue Buick we are bearing down on Kansas. He is using the touchstones of his ear and eye to wrap up the truth of his poems in a candy cellophane that is easily unfurled. Of course Charlie Parker is here; born in Kansas City, Kansas, and raised in the other Kansas, that one in Missouri. He is referenced, possibly a few times in the book, and you can hear his playing bouncing around the characters that inhabited Fairchild's formative years. Is that "Yardbird Suite" playing when Mrs. Hill comes to hide from her husband Lester, unhinged with threats of death, taken into the Fairchild home until the temperature drops? Patsy Cline, whose songs are mouthed by others in the back of the Buick, is this to call to mind the codeined back pains of Hank in his blue Cadillac? No Doz, Benzedrine, the cheaper and easier drugs than Parker's heroin dot the perimeter of some of the best pieces in the book, as does the music of Dexter Gordon,

Lester Young, Chris Connor, Django & Grappelli. Take this trip across the vast expanse, the auto part wreckage graveyards where the vessel we are in too, will surely land. The trunk is weighed down, giving the front end lift. Homeless newsprint rubs lightly on the windshield, like they could hear the authors in that tomb whispering to be let out. Rilke, Verlaine, Flannery O'Connor, as easy to read as tea leaves. He is a friend of yours that can jump from Gutenberg whose press we are nearly six centuries in on, has created a wealth and weakness of material, such that we too can only tread lightly on, scratch at the corners of. Later on, dispatches about Robert Rossen's imagined script for *Chinatown*, the Owens River dust, abandon borax plants, alkalized Mono lake, plays on chemistry, stereo versus quad, Oliver Sacks, St. Augustine, *The Book of The Dead*, and on and on for hours over coffee.

What was it that first took us from point A to point B? Did some awakening lead us on, these paths of illusion? Thinking the answer could be found if we could line up in order every truth ever written or played on a cheap knock off Victrola, some kind of magical compound? Was it the tornado or the locusts that would do us in, possibly supply the impetus to move away? Oh, your parents sang, to find a college in a coastal state. To fuck and bleed and cry and cum on someone else's dime, or worse yet, one with a high-end interest rate we are locked into for decades. All of these illusions built as a means just to make us all leave home. Fairchild is from Kansas, and he can't help but mention Oz at least in passing in his pages. His is the kind of poetry that, were it read aloud, would still ring true with real world attributes, not a floral rabbit holed animatic stuck in the amber of being clever. Save them clunky verses fortified with man-made GMOs and chemicals to the point that even in the fury of fire, we couldn't properly cremate the body of the thing. His writing could be sewn into the aching chorus of "Don't Wait Up For Me," that human pause before Chris Connor delivers the final line of the song, dreamlike. "Mood Indigo" with emptied champagne bottles rolling down cobblestone streets, Procul Harum, Tammy Wynette, again, all songs or artists that float around the beams of Fairchild's one collection of poetry mentioned here. Catch the fleeting moments, the tremble in the airwaves in his book on tape. Disneyland isn't for dreamers, death is for dreamers. Fairchild gets us near enough to that door. He whispers only that admittance, if not granted, is a fault of only our own making. Here is a car. Here is a destination. Can you marry the two of them and get out of the way of the headlights?

IDA COX
CHARLIE MANSON BLUES

I WAS BORN IN SOUTHERN CALIFORNIA just a
few days before the Manson murders. Sorry Ma, wasn't around
for the summer of love, got here just in time to get rashes and
welts while all of them troubling headlines about end times hit
the pavement. I can compare only what that mass panic must
have felt like to my June of '84 through August of '85 when
Richard Ramírez, the mass killer known as "The Night Crawler"
haunted two of my teenage summers. The air was turned off at
night; we didn't dare open the screenless windows for a breeze
knowing that he was out in the night, on the prowl. The media
would attach the AC/DC song "Night Prowler" to Ramírez. It
was reported that a still unknown and unnamed killer slunk into
houses via unlocked sliders and open windows to kill his prey.
Ultimately thirteen people were killed by his hands. When he
was captured in late August of 1985, there was the same sigh of
relief that I am sure was felt in all of Southern California upon
the capture of Manson and his clan years earlier. They got 'em;
I am not going to die. I hesitate to mention the names of any
killers or murderers or accomplices to life snuffers; they, not even
deserving of an unmarked grave. The two mentioned above are
both dead, after suffering illnesses that even the most vengeful,
death penalty leaning of you would have wished on their kind.

Billie Holiday sounded nothing like what I had imagined Billie
Holiday would sound like when I finally heard her after hearing
the name for some years, not long after Ramírez's capture. It must
have been a latter-era song I first heard on KPCC. It was a lush,
fully orchestrated number and hers was a sweet voice, well, you

know that voice. The BYG label had an "Archive of Jazz" series of LPs available as French imports. There were the larger names (Ellington, Armstrong, Bechet, and Waller) but also lesser known artist (Muggsy Spanier, The California Ramblers). Volume 23 showed up in the bargain section of my local record store, it was by Ida Cox. The cover listed two songs that caught my attention just above her picture and below her name: "Misery Blues" and "Coffin Blues." All of the script on the back cover is in French and all I could glean from the rest of the notes were that these recordings were from 1924-1928 with a portion of the lyrics of "Coffin Blues" written in English. I slapped side two on the turntable first; I wanted to tap directly into "Coffin Blues." Written by Aletha Dickerson and Rose Taylor, the song is everything I had imagined Holiday would be. Ida Cox had an otherworldly voice, but also the kind of pitch and style that you would imagine if you were thinking of 1920's blues recordings. The song has the ache that you would also infer from the title. Holy shit, one of the best blues songs ever written coupled with one of the best performances, not only by Cox, but also her husband Jesse Crump on the keys and Tommy Ladnier on the trumpet. Amazing.

Think of all of their pain and suffering. The hustling and undercover of dark pantomiming they had to employ to get to the speakeasy just to play and sing. Everything today is so easy, so easy I hear all them older folks sing. You ever been so broke and despondent that you couldn't crawl out of your bed to make coffee? Coffee for the open-hearted, apple scrubbed army of checker playing straights that have no easier game to play than the game of tripping you up on your way to some public bathroom? Things are never easy. 1800s, last century, or now. I was born in the summer of the Manson murders and I am sure that my death—and yours too—will occur in an equally ugly time space.

ALICE COOPER BAND
THE TESTICLES OF ALICE COOPER

THE FIRE IN THE CANYON was the final sparked ember. The last straw, serving to deliver us from out of there; the city, the suburbs, the urban municipalities, none of them met our needs now at hand. A marriage of retreat and chalkboard Etch A Sketch is what we desired more than anything then.

It started with just the dozen of us, in that 1962 VW Transporter, dialing in that combination—101 to the 10 to the 15 to the 395 and then landing on that final click off of the 190. Underground, seriously underground. Makeshift at first as we gathered from behind the bodegas and grocery store pallet remnants, cardboard, plastics, crow nest builders for the black sheep king to use in these endless holes dug in the dunes. Who would think to look under the ever-moving dunes? Who would think? Pressed board as load-bearing walls, battery- and solar-powered light sources, keep it all quiet, subterranean. Hanging from a nail, one of the lanterns filled up over night with what looked to be sludge water, dank and brown. Kerosene? Blood? In through the grains and the cardboard from discarded 48-count water bottle packaging and the newspaper and the thrift store sheets, glad bags and our triple flannel shirted bodies. Dune buggy cut off shorts, razor blades hidden between the canvas and sole of someone or other's tennies. Black juju, unholy threes, we were calling on anything for delivery from here once.

In our spandex shoelaces which, I would reflect on years later, we wore in the event that one of us did collect twenty or so shoelaces, we would then only be able to trampoline from that hanging tree, not still life in wait. It is an old story that is brought back into this world repeatedly. Everyone is looking for Arcadia, until a city in California is named after the place and reveals itself as just another blasé Adelanto or Garden Grove. Strict guidelines start seeping in like the light shafts and evening draft 'neath the lip of the door. Pecking orders, hierarchies, enemy lists... everything was there that you think, and it did in time reveal itself. With the precision of a two year dental hygienist, bending back just a few of the flits of a landed ladybug, so it could no longer fly, only survive. We had fire tests regularly. Susan couldn't swim, and poor Jim didn't know how to ride a bike, every night a different cruel show of throwing one in the well, the other on the trail naked on a Schwinn. We are the women and the men buried in the dunes, not by villagers, but by our own hands.

Groups are not teams. They are not built to work together. There is no clear goal, even if that stated goal is fortune or fame, making it. Making it is a joke, it isn't a score. How many athletes lose themselves in the rain after a red letter season? How many groups? Foster familied surgically sewn together limbs that don't belong that way. You can't see it, when you are in it and you don't feel it nor even hear it, all the talking in circles for days, mainly eves. Bum fuckToledodedo poetry in this counterfeit ashram. Holding séances, smearing blood on your high cheekbones at the gig, throwing dolphin bone necklaces to the girl in the third row with the cornrowed teeth; different circles, same fish. It is the individual you need to be mindful of, not the mob. Watch and listen to them as from a pulpit or into the Pye studio camera their end time screeds blare as they are beamed into the far flunken corners; caring less if you got reeled in by curiosity, late night drunken viewing irony or just the shit and giggle of the gilded set. Look at your feet when you are walking. Catch street names, off ramps, call boxes. If you are stranded don't eat, and drink any fluids that are not ample sparingly. In the eve, all of our nightmares are our own making, and in in our waking life, we cannot afford to sleep.

CAROLE KING
MACRAMÉ

TAPESTRY WAS THE SOUND of 1971, 1972 and 1973 in my household and millions of others in America. Not to be overly dramatic, but the fabric of the family falling apart was a huge theme in the Americas of the '70s. I was living then in that experimental world of single mothers raising their babies with the freshly minted non-shame of divorce. I was three in 1972, and the songs on *Tapestry* were spilling out from under the lip of my sister Loretta's door, into the hallway and then into the room that my brother and I shared. She didn't know that King had gone through a divorce in 1968 that would surely lend light to the songs on the record she would record in 1970 and release in 1971 (fittingly, her ex co-wrote three songs on the record). She couldn't know that Carole would go on record with three more divorces: City bandmate Charles Larkey, whose bass playing is amply present on *Tapestry;* then followed in 1978 by Rick Evers, a friend of Don Henley, who died of a cocaine overdose at a shooting gallery. Don't forget about Teepee Rick who, after 5 years of marriage, called it quits in 1987.

We are all trying to find home, and on "Home Again," King delivers some easy relatable lines at the song's beginning, but tucked in the corner of the song, there it is, the mark of what an incredible songwriter King is. "Snow is cold, rain is wet/Chills my soul right to the marrow." "It's Too Late" is another E ticket beckoning the exhausted to attempt to go it alone. There is Beck's father David Campbell on the viola on "Way Over Yonder" and "You've Got a Friend," years before his son's own gilded break up album that Campbell would have strings stretched over, 2002's confessional *Sea Change*. Sure the trappings of James Taylor and Russ Kunkel are on the record, but check Merry Clayton's backing vocals on "Way Over Yonder," and that is her again on "You've Got a Friend." "Beautiful" is a song that begins with a prayer. Advice that we give ourselves, and then scoff at as we brush off the hastily-eaten morning crumbs in the rearview. You can hear Aretha Franklin whispering here and there across the record if you listen closely.

King is, of course, a national treasure. Her brand of Laurel Canyon granola is superior to that of Norman Greenbaum, Melanie, Stephen Stills and other writers of gooey feel good now pay in the morning contemporaries of hers. She had kids to raise, a cat to take care of and other pressing things to tend to after the late night barefoot Persian Isfahan wool ruggery spills of Loggins & Messina. I am talking about a woman who wrote "He Hit Me (And It Felt Like A Kiss)" with her husband upon hearing that their babysitter was being beat up by her ne'er-do-well boyfriend. She would love to sit and chat with you about decoupage and yarn-lined party trays, but she has a slightly loopy James Taylor on the line and the kids are crying for milk.

THELONIOUS MONK
NORCO 1982

C AN YOU IMAGINE how tiring it must be to have to talk to idiots about their dissertations; their knee-scraped half-cooked thesis, for one who was born with a language that years of study will never allow them entry? The French interviewer who, after having played an original that stands as one of the most unique and important pieces of 20th century, hurls hot lamps and condescending questions at him? He had just gotten off of the stage, sweating profusely and in another place, and this fool has the wherewithal to mess with him? Monk, you were graceful, shrugging the interpreter's questions off to the side of things. Maybe not wanting to appear difficult as your reputation had hardened by that time, or maybe that fuselage that had been in flight for most of your life had been kicked and beat upon so often, that this meant nothing to you. Your kids, in one documentary or other that I have seen, talk about when you came home from touring. You were exhausted. You would play cards with them on the bed and tell them to imagine that the bed is a boat, afloat right now, there is no flooring, no doorway, and we are here, now, on this little landing. Any parent can relate to the exhaustion of not being able to pull it together to get out of bed. When this kind of behavior is attributed to mental illness, or your singular playing style to unlearnedness, it calls to play why the public is so hesitant of those assigned the duty of the critic. There are thousands of critics of the arts whose very art is on display only in this cage. The better ones know that it is a game of catch as catch can 22s. That to be critical does not equate with being reprehensible. Those stumble in the light bottom shelf critics are not doing God's work, and goddamn if most of them didn't stumble into their positions as a means of escape from the droll day-to-day of God's lesser work. You hang around anywhere long enough, you learn that you need to protect your own. There are forces that were built only to digest and discard, move on along to the next debate. Forgive them all. But most of all, keep this in your back pocket. Most of the beloved and in retrospect highest praised artists in the highest of high to the lowest of low circles are the artists that could not be taught. That whir winded their way onto something by endless hours alone in a vacuum; self-taught techniques by their own hands, all their own way. There is no teacher that can find your voice. A good teacher will shine some lights there in a few corners, try to steer you away from the garland, but the truth of it is that we don't have much in the way of free will when it comes to the gifts that come naturally to us, and the many deficits that we endlessly work to compensate for. The establishments are filing resumes under your door daily, epistles that spell out why they are the path, the light, the only escape. Schools, religions, bureaucracies, the places you need to go if you want to know the easily learned version of wisdom, spirituality & community. Norco 1982, no sidewalk and a rosary through the window, we don't need it right now, we are OK and wish you only the best.

THE
REPLACEMENTS
ATTIC FREE

MOST DAYS, I dress in the dark before the sunrise. I work alone for a few hours, before anyone else sets foot in the six thousand square feet of this building. You can see me through the two-way glass in my tiny closet-sized office at 6:45, maybe I am typing, maybe mouthing imagined lyrics to a Roswell Rudd trombone. Later in life, he could be found on a cruise line playing for passengers with no knowledge of the sides he had laid down in the '60s and the '70s and even then, before he died, he couldn't care less if you had even heard of him. That was Fay Victor bending her vocals to his trombone when he, at 81, recorded his final album, *Embrace*, a sweet farewell to those closest to him. It might not be until 9:35 or so in the morning before I catch sight of myself, washing my hands in the mirror after pissing, see some crumbs on my chin, an inside-out shirt, deodorant tracks up the left side, hair matted down on my forehead, I might catch sight then, or these physical shortcomings might be visible to the first person that rings the bell for deliveries; the mail, the hostile investor in the lot just west of us, maybe one of our good-natured employees. Those are the interruptions, most mornings. I see gray coming in, my Midwest roots, and I don't mind. My mom's side of the family was raised on a farm in Argyle, Minnesota. My aunt made a dare to jump from the limbs of a tree onto a bull; my mom would wring the neck of a chicken and bring it to my grandmother to cook. Me? It broke my heart when my wife and I had to exhaust pipe them chickens we raised from chicks on our driveway after the raccoons got to them. There was Millie, the runt of that litter that the other two pecked and fucked with that died first, even after the admonishments and separations and seventy-two other tricks we employed to guard our sweet black sheep. We are farmers, we are hillbillies. You can't get between nature; you, after all, are the intruder, the weed through the asphalt, the living thing opening wide for their carcinogenic sprays.

When you glance for just a moment, and know deep within you that the person before you on the subway or the mass transit Omni Trans, or the cross walking slo-mo is a minute part of you, well, you might just hit the brake. Stop your mind from racing. Stop dot stop - from being a quick flash generator of thought. That little part of me comes from Minnesota, where my Aunt Lucille, on a stopover visit with our band, walked us with her husband around the lake and through the basement to see everything they had collected of worth, glass encased. Where my Aunt Joyce, after serving with the Peace Corps, entered into a mixed-race marriage at a time in the early '70s when that kind of thing could have ostracized both sides of that family line. Where my Aunt Eileen would be there in a heartbeat, offering salvation at every blood red stop sign, would joke with me about her stash of pills in her 80s. "When the mind goes, down the hatch them pills follow." Raised in the middle of nowhere, you need to be self-reliant. You have to be able to take your lumps for every decision you make. Strong women run in my family, and men too. Raymond? Milton? They were the hilarious brothers of the clan. Death has to do that thankless work that no one wants to do; took one from an electrocuted ladder, the other from melanoma. So it is with Midwesterners. Don't take their kindness and good-natured hearts as some kind of throwback, naïve melody. They work hard, incredibly hard, to retain that sensibility. Point, snicker, make fun, and laugh three beats after they have left the room. You think they lack for hearing? Later, you can marvel at their generosity, when you are older probably, just passed the middle age sight lines. Maybe you will reflect about the chip on their shoulder then. Hell, just look at how they react. Bob Dylan, Prince, and The Replacements—all from my home state—dressing you down, sometimes in the most subtle of ways, other times with a brick to yer face, you think we ain't seeing these things? You think we are just going to take it lying down? We kill our pets by hand when they are maimed. We shovel shitloads of white snowflakes out the driveway, just so we can appear before you.

In California, with a pool in my backyard, I wake up by 6 every AM. I mow the lawn to the song of all of my neighbor's gardeners. I am pruning the citrus trees that Catherine makeshift smudge-potted during a few freezing Southern California eves with me. That is us—fixing the pipe fittings, deadheading any flowerings, mulching & laboring & lifting. Midwestern grays, snow blanketing the light. Every morning we try to get as much done as we can before sunrise. We don't know how we look, and were we to see ourselves in a bathroom mirror, well, we wouldn't really care enough to stare. I remember a college graduate that couldn't spell, trying to school me in art. Two brass rings with holes for the forward thinking to slip through. The holes in my shoes, I wouldn't remember come morning, that those were there from the night before when we shot ourselves to sleep.

TROUBLE
PSALM TEN

CHRISTIAN METAL, THERE IS such a vast world of topics for the writer of Christian metal songs to tap into. God knows, you could write an epic song about building Noah's Ark that would not reveal itself until the last couplet that this unimaginable task bestowed on this poor blue collar Joe was to gather couples of every persuasion and house them safely for a journey if that were your forté. By no means can I envision the song being any good, but it would be epic in the same way that I can only imagine Jethro Tull's *Thick As a Brick* or the film *Gone With The Wind* are purported to be having made a deal with myself as a teenager to never, ever, under any circumstance listen to that record nor watch that movie. Maybe that record and that film are incredible, and perhaps that Noah's Ark Song of yours, too, will be one of the great unseen/unheard classics whose spine will never be touched by this lacking of time/loss of sight judgmental fool.

Trouble's debut LP on white vinyl bests any other classic Christan metal release that I have thus heard. Stryper, the trinity of Neon Cross, White Cross and The Barren Cross—all of whose music I must have heard while listening to Jim Ladd's *Mighty Metal Hour* that aired Friday nights on KMET—none of them have anything on Trouble. Others, who were lost to me, I can't fairly measure. There was Holy Soldier who swear that they are the most important and identifiable Christian rock band in rock 'n' roll history, but I have yet to check that box. Hell, I am only aware of them as I saw their record in the used bin a few months back in the record store. There are now a slew of hard rock Christian bands, just as there are Christian chocolatiers and Christian macramé entwiners. It is an equal opportunity world and being such, it is only right that Christian Science Satanists and every other sect have to drive buses and dig ditches like the rest of us. In 1984, there were only a few alternatives to the straight boy metal. There was Leather Angel, the female quartet, Hellion, and Bitch whose lead singers were female; Judas Priest's Rob Halford, whom I argue was never in the closet, his lexicon of lyrics was maybe the first clue. King Kobra, whose drummer Carmine Appice played in Rod Stewart's band before a short stint with Ozzy that led him to cash in on the metal craze with a band of him and four blonde bros—one of whom, lead singer Mark Free, has since transitioned and is Marcie Free. Metal is often given a bad rap for a narrow world view. Dig deeper to see it isn't so.

I recall Jim Ladd playing "Bastards Will Pay," the lead-off cut on side two of Trouble's debut record, and wondering—if they were practicing Christians, how could they sing such a sentiment? Today of course, the evangelical world has no problem telling all us divine-less bastards that we will pay, but back then it may have been housed in a kinder wrapper. "Sinners will pay," but bastards? I stayed tuned to hear who sang this song, there were groans from my brother and I as Ladd mispronounced Metallica as "Metal-ee-ka," who were also in that set, but he did get back to the fact that "Bastards Will Pay" was by a band called Trouble. Ladd's long hair and sexist on-air persona was as close as KMET had to foot the bill for one of their DJs to have a metal show, but he was obviously Dick Clarking here, swimming in a pool for commerce's sake, not a love of this new music that he couldn't quite comprehend. Nonetheless, Ladd was charming in the same way as KROQ DJ Rodney Bingenheimer mispronouncing Throwing Muses as "Throwing Mooses" or Fugazi as "Fuh-gozzy." Trouble's debut record holds up today where so many other metal records don't. These guys had their back up against a wall and were certainly made fun of in the metal clubs they frequented for their religious beliefs. You can hear it amply present in the record's take no prisoners onslaught of lean metal. From Psalm Ten: Break the arm of the wicked man; call the evildoer to account for his wickedness that would not otherwise be found out. They mean it, Maaan.

TALK TALK

CORINTHIANS

GROUP C, IN THE HIGH 40s, awaiting the boarding of the plane. Sure, A & B are here, but I don't feel as though I am waiting with them. I am waiting on them. Like I did in my twenties in restaurants to make ends meet; like I did in my teens for adolescence to move me out from myself. I had fallen asleep for just a few seconds in one of them mercilessly uncomfortable tandem slings in the lobby of the departing, having caught the eye of a fellow employee, not quite friend of mine. Maybe it was sleep, maybe it was feigning. Don't look at me. Don't sit by me, Paul. My right ankle resting on the inappropriately named stainless steel leg whose bottom clasp was mounted to the floor. A workaday will that made sure some twenty-six years ago that not only would this chair remain stationary in this low-end editing room, but any fool sitting here would be uncomfortable enough to surrender any concentration they might have mustered to do something other than passenger the hours away. You see us all, folded newspapers, bookmarks slid into novels, unengaged phone slouchers whiling the whirr of their machines to sleep. A credit here then, to that Mike Davis brand of mean-spirited workmanship that would disallow sleep for the homeless. I stare out the window thinking of that tour of an airport my class went on in the fourth grade—Jumbo Jets and 747s and my favorite at the time, an Airbus, here with new skins and innards. Kids don't get tours of airports no more. Keep them kids out of any public places. Sitting restlessly, I wander from the concept to creation nightmare of this trap. Cottage cheese popcorn drop ceilings and lo-fi PA systems spill down to the matte tile designed to hide filth. Are they so knowledgeable about the most common colors of spills that their committee wisely chose a mauve-veined tan tile? Mauve and tan to hide the coffee, the bile, the dirt and dried blood. Will that camouflage most things?

Stay occupied. Don't look up. Play games of the mind. Was this airport built by non-union hacks? Will our pilot come from the same lineage? Rod Serling monkeys on the wing, not hurting anyone, just simply doing their thing. Once in the early nineties, at a local supermarket in a state of exhaustion, I saw the corpse of Julio Iglesias on the cover of People magazine. Maybe I was seeing the same kind of thing, my mind sputtering out useless translations of what was before it. Sometimes you can't turn off the think, can't get out of a loop of your own making. Hell, I just wanted to get into the vessel and rest my head on the pulled-down shade of that window. I imagined putting on my noise-canceling headphones. No small talk, no divorcee in a religious fervor next to me, please, just a window seat near the tail, that then would have been an unbelievable deliverance. Snake handlers, professional travelers, carry on pillow-necked with our sandals instead of shoes. You want to turn us into Jesuits, or worse yet, halfwit *Match Game* Gene Rayburn fools? Skinny microphoned drunken buffoons, afraid of the next step, of the clatter in mind of the starboard. Right, I forgot I was trying to get on the air bus, forgot where I was with my boarding pass blues alit on my phone.

"I can't seem to talk about the things that bother me," Paul told me at last year's employee Christmas party. Hell, who says those kinds of things at a party? Bored then, boarding a plane now, I can only wonder what the right thing to say then would have been. Ah, don't bring it up. There is a different language between the two of you and not a thing of weight is ever on display when we have a conversation. The surroundings they change, like hallway carpets in hotels get replaced, or overhead light fixtures. It doesn't matter the change, it is as close to nothing as you will ever visit. Nod, and get on, and sit by the emergency door, Paul. You can guide us all out of the wreckage with your waterproof Dick Tracy watch and SPF 100 ghost sheen.

The two of us, we have only a few things in common of note. We were in a band together for three years a couple of decades back, and now we work at the same office, for the same company. We are in different departments, and do completely different jobs mirroring our previous relationship. I was not curious about the keyboard then and what you played, I am not curious about the keyboard now and your interoffice milquetoast missives that now and again come my way. They are, by their very nature, supposed to be built that way. I understand. My CC'd whining reminders are not the work of some top drawer scribe. They read like refrigerated post-it notes by a spurned roommate, carrying along with them the same disinterest and impersonal touches.

Do we have to sit in the same row? Four-flush friendship, talk about the office, and judge those before us. Some people are able to skip from young adulthood to middle-aged artist with ease, I mean, from the age of 20 to 23, all the sudden, metamorphosed. We didn't even see a cocoon. Just a pupa, then some fully-formed things breaking up the ground around our feet. Or maybe it was just at our feet in that cramped studio apartment of Mark's where it was all coming so quick that canvases and drying ink was resting upon, next to and abutting everything. Do you not recall, or maybe it meant nothing to you? You split before he became the laughing stock. Carrying on, after trial lawyers, bean counters, abacus rosaries, holy water, and a whole myriad of dead ends lit the pathway out. How many magic tricks can one person possess? How many miracles do we need to feed on before we leave in peace? With a tonic that was equal parts recluse and fanned at obscurity, into the ether there was still delivered one last missive, stark and brief, before retiring to the countryside of a new Jerusalem.

We move and we travel and we speak. In silence his second solo album keeps company with himself only. I had heard he has a couple of kids, farting around with a stack of books here, a grocery list there, tending to that of the day. There is no mystery to be unsheathed, no great reveal. It is not a life of nirvana for any of us. Not a path of knowingness, and not because there wasn't a lack of trying. We are the architects of our days, the creators, the gods of malaise. Here in this airport, and here, on this plane, projecting only as far as my arm can reach to the inflight options of air and trays of Glad-wrapped Snyder of Hanover pretzels, diet sandpaper magazines. The astral is not here with me, just a vacant horizon. We are still four hours away from the tarmac. We were there, and now we are in flight. If the credits rolled right here, you could pin some score just under it to ease our infantile landing. Don't think about where you are headed or what was left behind. Here, here is where the two of us are right now, long gone in the friendly skies. I love storybook endings.

EARL SWEATSHIRT
WE NEED MILK

THE ONE TWO PUNCH of *Doris* followed by *I Don't Like Shit, I Don't Go Outside* might be the hardest hit to the body since *808s* and *Dark Fantasy* by Kanye West. Vulnerable, claustrophobic records that drip with sorrow even as they stew in a homemade brew of braggadocio. I imagine what was going on in the mind of the sixteen/seventeen-year-old Thebe Neruda Kgositsile after his mom sent him to a boarding school for at-risk teens, packed him up to Samoa; was that as far away a place as she could think of? Was it then that he worked beatless on the rhymes of *Doris*? The track "Chum" dances around the state of things between the former Thebe rechristened Earl Sweatshirt from an Odd Future mixtape named *Earl* some years earlier. "Burgundy" addresses his poet father (deceased) and the passing of his grandmother. The kid should have instead—on some shitty twenty piece scratch paper pad with the image, name and address of a married real estate couple on the header—written innocuous things like "Mom, back by 10" or "We Need Milk" or maybe "Janis called, said she'll try you later." I can live without another great record. I can survive without another novel that delves into and catches the honest reflection of the stark truth if in turn it means that the writer had a life without an overabundance of sorrow. All of them successful artists, neglecting their children, husbands and wives, I would swear off of them truly if it meant the blood and gut narrators would have a better life. Living in the shadow of a gated coma unity though, it does serve us to hear the howl of others late into the eve. Someone else out in the moors of fog and headlights, lost and wounded, reminding us that this flavor of pain is valuable too. Nearly every time I play this record and its follow up, I hold out hope that someone from the kid's family is there for him now. If that is what middle age does to you, I hate to ponder what my reflections on Pasolini's *Salò* will bring to my mind should I live to be ninety-five.

OFF!
FLICK OF THE SWITCH

THE CINEMATOGRAPHER CALLED IT a broken home. I don't know what she meant by broken. We still lived there. We answered the phone, did our laundry, attempted homework under the weight of the watch over. I meant to tell her before she pulled out the junk drawer, don't do that. Some party guest pissed inside of that. I don't know who or when, but I know, nonetheless. We sit and we make plans, crossed out Etch-a-Sketch, thumbed-up hitch a rides. I cannot for the life of me, recount all of the times my wife she told me in passing, "you should leave me now." Now before it gets worse than this, before it weighs upon us, before it erases what went before us. Some things just catch on fire. There is no rhyme to them, they were sitting right there in the dark the entire time, just waiting for a spark to catch on them so they could then reveal themselves, their true selves, the self that had been guarded nearly all of this time. Is someone near that can turn on the light, explain to me the plight of all of my present that is backed up against the future? If they could, would it then be a quickly spraypainted sign that reads: "This closed road furthering notice, until then...caution."

You were one of them, one of us, taking every bankruptcy in hand; never one to make demands, excepting them once in a whiles. Once when you had to tell the promoter you weren't going to man that card table, signing would-be landfill, glass casing digital postings. Those kinds of things hold no weight. No, wait, I am almost there. A flick of the switch would blow you sky high, on the radio, I am, listening with my twelve-year-old, I am. You can call all of what we have broken. You can define the terms, attempt for years to undo the damage, make whole the halves that you are left with instead of being present. I'd rather Raymond Pettibon than Greg Ginn, better to Mike Watt than Jello Biafra, Watt was amplifying the darkness inside of him. He, then, was painting. First with his best friend, then with his wife. Dos, dos times two, quatro, ocho, Sesenta y cuatro. Why can't you? Maybe tomorrow. Why can't you, this sorrow, Econoline away all of this weight? All of this sorrow and all of this weight away. It is never too late in life to form a band with your friends. It is never too late in life to turn on the amps, switch on the fuse box, let them black cords from your amp to your guitar crawl around and trip you up in a garage. We both looked at each other, with that knowing nod. Now this, this is living.

LORD INVADER
6 TEXTS

1. Maybe it's not enough, an entry into lost diaries. An uncle of bus stops mapping a way for you from him away. His vocal pipes are filled with lye and vinegar. Still, you come when at dusk he calls for you. Another grunt groan dinner date. Pecking bread from some fuckface's hand that can't stop talking to me about all of his favorite bands, who sings along to Pandora, no, kid, that box there isn't open.

2. "The city is ours tonight" - smiley face, childlike emoting.

3. You appear three weeks later in Anaheim California Adventure with your Las Vegas bankrupted hamper holding all the dirtied clothes that you supposed I would know what to do with. Keep them in a hefty bag, side of road them, and delete them with every other unanswered thing.

4. The last late bus. Missed carriages. Shoeless princeless princess needing a tetanus shot from the sharpened teeth you begged open, the diseased legs veined spider swollen. I couldn't fit you in my car, not with all of your luggage thick from the rains. We'll have to walk the last few miles, carry what we can, and jettison what we can't. There used to be all-night diners now there are only Denny's and IHOPs, they are like set dressings appearing as restaurants appear on TV. Hot, stuffy, clanky graveyards, the dead aren't yet buried, we are just having a watered down warm up. We couldn't then agree on where to go, so here we sit. These are not the places I would choose to go to smoke and drink coffee. I'd just as soon drive through, sitting here in these bucket seats so we didn't have to face each other with something less than wonder. We are

two deep in a vinyl booth with an empty chair at the head. Is the hostess making a sick joke at our expense? Housing for us even more emptiness? Back from the bathroom and you crystal balling your phone. No one is going to call. No one is there. The food arrives, we can barely eat. You now barely eat anyway. But you drink, and you smoke and you must think. I just can't really tell because you are staring down, not listening or talking.

5. When you finally found her, and all of her bloody spoons, razors hidden in rags, you recalled, and later told me, that they used to say that about you: "She was so sharp." Now years later, well on your way to becoming some dulled inconsequential knife hidden in the junk drawer. Don't come by anymore, I ain't answering the door. The door to danger at my place. A relative hum, misfitting bulbs in the hall, dull pitched paint singing sunken to me every time I make it to the bathroom stall. The shared phone by the walker, old *TV Guides* that ponder the silver age stacked neatly next to the folding chair. The age of yesterday doesn't change; it is blanketed under the frost of June's rent and October's bondsmen with their reassuring smiles. Lord, invader, you are one and the same. No rum and coke, just some low rent apocalypso music on the FM. To no one in particular, I am talking to. Don't come by anymore. I ain't answering the what for. How about instead we happy ending it? Leave it on the patio, the danger at my place. Hope that someone steals it in the midday.

6. "Anyone can be found, regrettably" -smile like, like a child's face.

ESQUERITA
SINGS THE OBLIVIANS
SONGBOOK

ERIC FRIEDL HAS GIVEN HIS LIFE over to junk
culture. He co-owns an indie record store in Memphis which
may have started in tandem with his zine "Wipe Out" that was
published in the early to mid-'90s. Things got a little hairy once
the record store soon became a record label as well, sharing the
same Goner name. The first release arrived media mail to me
in 1994, Japan's Guitar Wolf shared all of the aesthetics of the
magazine and what would come to be the band Eric was in, The
Oblivians. Cheap mimeograph glue stick slaps with staples, he
took the zine and with his band gave it the soundtrack that it
deserved. Garage rock minus the bullshit schlock of retro fonts
or gimmicky stage outfits. The Oblivians have not put out a bad
record, their release with Quintron on the organ kills as does
their 2013 reunion record *Desperation*. Take a look at all the
incredible limbs that the members of the band grew into after
their break up: Reigning Sound, The Dutch Masters, guest stints
with Tav Falco, production and collaborations with a myriad of
underground legends and see how they were able to shoo away
the webs and the worries of staid boredom. Call your dead mom's
beeper if you disagree, she'll get back to you what you deserve.

BILL FAY AVEC MERZBOW

MARITIME FAREWELL

A CHRISTIAN & A NOISE MAKER walk into a chapel. They call one an unbeliever, and the other complicit in deceit. Bill Fay, whose gentle songs lead me to believe that he would take the leftover after Merzbow made his choice of the two, is one of them unbelievable stories. Fay, after all, had the wherewithal to put out a pair of fantastically uneven records in 1970 and '71 and not release a third for a quarter century. For one as talented and curious as him, it is a true feat. How do you not keep going? Merzbow, whose every squeal and blip must have by now been revealed to us as he, at this writing, nears his 300th release. How does he stop? Two curious minds making the most extreme of decisions. Choose filmmakers Robert Bresson or Terence Malick, whose films came into the world meditatively, with probably more imagined labor than what you would perceive was true of those as prolific as Fassbinder or D.W Griffith. Is it the value in the lack of early work over two decades from Malick, or those late in life poetic meditations that, from 2010 to the roaring 2020s, came in such a Godspeed fashion that it was hard to keep track of the spokes for his viewers? Are you able to move from 80 mph to a merged exit in a seventieth of a mile in enough time without killing anyone?

My heart goes out to the modern day artist who has to press hands, kiss babies, be at a merchandise booth to greet you, stray from offending any and all looking down on her from a big cloud, asking of the artist to change, though not too radically as to lose us, the mass of backsliders. Magus, do something new, again, again and again. Now, just like before, just like before. We are no longer patrons of the arts, because we don't really support the arts or the artist. There is no mechanism to fund failed experiments, lackluster side roads or the go save me plea of trying to find your way out of the wilderness. We are out here, all faceless en masse with little time and little means with which to support all that is available to us. There are too many writers and singers and directors and painters and sculptors and dancers and pre-postmodern side steppers. We can't fit you all in our hearts or minds. What choices did you leave us?

A good friend of mine has an older model Royal typewriter from which she has removed the ribbon. Every morning, for 15 minutes, she feeds the same piece of paper into the carriage and types out whatever comes to her. This piece of paper may be reused sixty, seventy times before it becomes impossible to reload. Sure, missed days from illness, travel etc., but even when there was nothing to think or say, descriptions of modal scales for the piano, oil versus inks, hair in the place of clothing etc., would be pounded out on that keyboard for none but her sanity and her ritual. For my birthday one year, she gave me 25 ratty old sheets of paper in one of them Oxford twin pocket folders. Five years of thought for no one to own and no one to see. We should all be so lucky.

Luciano Berio
Cinque Vision

MAYBE NOT THIS SONG, and then maybe not the next one, but I hope one of them will be yours. Here, or overhead, from a draconian jukebox that thins all hope down to coins as thin as dimes, ah, I will take them and their 18 cents of change from your eyes; any salt-rolled pain caught up in a wave that tugged at you shoreless, boated you oreless. I will write a letter to the editor and implore her, remind her, there is always a way back. Even here, in your torn up pajamas, well, in a stained shirt and shorts presenting, presenting, only me or only you, that will do. Grip that rope. Steady yourself in a sinking U-boat because you never know, you just never know. I recall my forehead cracked in bathroom porcelain, but not the following day. I recall you breaking a window to get into my apartment. I remember the whiplash of being spun so fast for so long that we couldn't see straight or steady our heads to focus. Did I, then, hold on? Did I hold on, and if so, for how long? Or was I gone? Was I gone? You wouldn't say. You wouldn't say. Maybe the wrong song in a book inscribed to the wrong name, the wrong spelling. Sheela, nah, my name is Sheila you would tell me. But all the same, after all that boredom and violence, still we stand, upright in a penny arcade. We appear on a dimed up nickelodeon sound stage. Right before your eyes, right before your eyes, we did then appear before flying away. Before flying away.

It was Mussolini, whose army you served unwillingly that, unbeknownst to him, changed your fate. With that injured hand, a piano player you would never make. It was your first wife's voice married to your electronics, and then a second wife in Oakland of all places (what the hell is an Italian doing in Oakland, my grandmother, who loved Mussolini, would say). It is the age old story that is sweet and trite, until it happens to you. The pain and misery of not being able to pursue your hopes and dreams only to land on some kind of unbroken ground that you are allowed to author; to dust up and sleep bag-style it at night; to drag an accordion to the opera halls, a poor Italian boy's piano as it is known in my family, hung around the neck of one of the string players. I do more than just play the accordion, see? Berio, himself, should be regarded as a poet as well as any other facet of his life you would care to name and ascribe to him. Read any one of his interviews, his defining, or lack thereof, of terms, are often a means of not describing his music or his art, but can often be read as directives on how to build a house, or how to house a soul. Sure, beard strokers and eyelash batters may dot the circumference of his recordings, showboating their vocabularies with a high-priced pedantic steel, but simply open the sliding door, usher those thoughts out, and welcome a tour guide who is attempting to show you windows made out of blood, hearths filled with inflammable drawers, go on, store your popsicles and ice cream in that while I take you further down the hallway for a tour of the bathtub made of herbal bricks. It is playful and wide open to misinterpretation. That is how things are when they are newly birthed.

TIM BUCKLEY
LOOK AT THE OCTOGENARIAN

BORN ON VALENTINE'S DAY 1947, dead in the summer of 1975. His is the voice that would have been fascinating to hear as it neared elderly status. As the elasticity gave way to age, would there have been a deeper ache, that forever plaintive delivery of his with clipped wings? Like those records on Pablo by our aging jazz greats as they moved up the ladder to their sixth, seventh, then eighth decade. A Jerome Kern songbook. A Patty Waters duets record. A return to the stripped down folk of two mics direct to analog tape. For all the credit/groans that David Bowie elicits for his changeling ways, Buckley—though no slouch when it comes to his influence on the music world today and in the days since his death—was forever searching. Folk, soft psych, free jazz explorations, funk, butt boogie rock, balladeer. So many of our favorite artists are celebrated for that one silver sliver era, usually five years, a window five years in length. We may get drawn into the deep end and turn over every early recording and/or visit every latter-era film or installation, but there are few whose conversation with us is sustained for a lifetime. Here are thousands of your friends. You can't stay intimate with all of them. You wish them only the best, as there is only so much time to catch a meal, much less reveal all the intimate details of their and your waking life, in concert, with one another. Some of us just passed through the halls for four years, had a small affinity for one another. Others, into the fire, for decades, as close as tongues and teeth. Very few, outside of our family, do we ride with for the duration, for as long as we can. Take every mistaken exit, land unexpectedly in some graveyard or fiftieth anniversary.

I run my finger over the spine of thousands of LPs, land on The Fall. Are there forty records here? The summer before lead singer/lyricist/agitator Mark E. Smith died, I played through every Fall record I owned, one a day until I had exhausted them. Some titles were CD only, so add some other weird live releases, the fourth repackaging of some EPs and the odd side projects— like Von Südenfed or D.O.S.E.—and I had two months of aural work before me. One record every day. July seventh, it was just the four track "Peel Sessions" from their November 27th, 1978 recorded set that would be broadcast a month later in that same year. A little less than a decade later it would be released by the Strange Fruit label. We got to hear how Mark sounded as he cozied up to being sixty years of age. Magnificent. Like Billie before him, hers a Strange Fruit of another kind, them missing teeth and years of hard drink and drugs malformed those voices, which led two singers from two entirely different worlds to have to make artistic choices they couldn't have made at twenty-three. Them notes they couldn't hit, those Smith squeals that were no longer possible.

Buckley and Smith are both artists of whom I own nearly all of their recorded work, and return to it all fairly equally, not favoring any particular era. For them, I had the time for whatever they wanted to tell me just then. In the case of The Fall, in real time, each record coming out with news of the high and low, and where he had been since we last talked.

A stilled voice in its youth is celebrated, for there is no age, not as much room for stumbles and mistakes. The mistakes that are made are turned over again and again by some, looking for imaginary avenues that might have been gone down. If Buckley had lived, he may have very well have exhausted the musical terrain that he was due to be traveling upon, but there certainly would have been some interesting returns to where he had once been, by one who in his music life was inquisitive and fearless.

JOHN CALE

PARIS 1999

D ECEMBER 11, 2012 El Rey Theatre Los Angeles, California: I never buy band shirts, merchandise seldom (a hand-held Sparks "Kimono My House" fan, sure). Passing the lobby and into the venue, Catherine suggests buying me a John Cale shirt as an early Christmas present. Sure, why not. The shirt doesn't have Cale's name on it and is a fairly obtuse design. We then head to the foot of the stage, maybe two rows back, hard to make out the actual line of demarcation as it is a sloppy, mostly middle-aged crowd that is a bit drunk and wearing the work day blues from being stuck in a cubicle or on their feet all day. Cale opens with three songs that all have their hands in the literary realm: "Hedda Gabler," "Captain Hook" and "The Hanging." "Hedda Gabler," Cale is kind of looking at Catherine and I, some folks around us, sussing out the crowd. "Captain Hook," he is noticeably staring at Catherine, kind of odd as in the thousands of shows we have been to, even at the smallest of shows with only a dozen folks in the audience, I don't recall anyone making this kind of studied, relentless eye contact. Third song, "The Hanging," Catherine is blushing and looking down at her feet. This continues for the duration of the set. I remember a friend who played a show with Cale relating that Cale was passing out condoms backstage, wishing all to get lucky after the show. Granted, my wife is gorgeous, a striking six-foot-tall lady, but what the hell, John Cale, could you not see my kisses on her nape or arm around her? You think you can Nabakov her out from under me for one night of splinters and dried-up beer foam backstage? Later in the set, playing songs off of your latest record, "I Wanna Talk 2 U" and "Nookie Wood" strike me as direct come-ons to her as you continue to leer. There was a lesson to be learned years ago when, as a fourteen-year-old, I had tickets to an Ozzy and Ratt show at the Long Beach Arena. Even then, as my feet were just shy of sliding into punk rock, I was dumb enough to buy a Ratt T-shirt before their set. After their set, I returned to the merch booth and asked to exchange it for a "Bark At The Moon" shirt that I don't recall ever wearing. Have you ever seen Ratt live? It is one of the most forgettable things you can ever do. John Cale? I still wear the shirt once in a while, and sometimes it chafes my tits, but it reminds me that even those that haven't spoken to my wife, even the most whorey of the whores can see that she is something to be admired. Not sure if I am more of a lover or a fighter, but I am truly sorry John because the doggone girl is mine.

THE MYDDLE CLASS
SILVERWOOD AND ELEVENTH

HERE, IN THE OLD HOUSE. The old middle class, the orange groves that housed the quarters for the hands. Slot machine sacrifice. Here is something for something else we can ill afford. The pump organ heater, as archaic and draconian as them silent film projectors. You gotta really push down on the pedals there to make any breath, and you have to put on a few shirts, a sweater, a jacket and a few quilts to get through the eves. Here now, the house appears bigger than when I lived there. Its oppressive heat in July, tacky fresh paint slapped on to cherry puff and hide all that the new owners think went on when we lived there. Yes, I would like to visit and be a tourist. I am ready to hear all about its history from a bleach-toothed docent. I don't want the abridged recorded headphone version; I want it live, from her mouth to my eyes as I square up what I know against what she says. Breast ploughs, wooden horse hames, muckrakes and scythes—these are the tools of modern day nightmares, once used to get down deep beneath the scalp of the earth. Pull up them meat fruits—chard, daikon, savoy cabbage, turnips & kohlrabi. This is the language of my elders. I see these things now only employed in big screen nightmare twist ups.

Well, it was probably a twist up and a nightmare then as well, under the roots of the present. Some circular Argyle farm that was burned down, that broke the back of my grandfather again and again. Red ant hills in the backyard. Soil that filled in the backyard like a gum line built to only prop up teeth. Rocks the size of potatoes, rocks the size of newborn babies. Good luck getting anything to grow back there. Up and down that block, they made it home. The worst of things couldn't trump that we were now on one of them American coasts. Pushing up to keep the slide from claiming us. Take a tour of that ghost ship now. Razed to house a stretch of laundromats and pizza chains. The latest wave of immigrants have arrived. They have been given our rusted up shackles to restrain them from getting too far, too fast. From the Midwest, from the east, to California, both sides of our family fled. Out west, where the Brooklyn Dodgers are now housed in silicone reefs that regenerate their hurts daily, miraculously. I am a ghost in their presence, I am living, but I am not sure that it beats what they are doing in the forever aftering. Go on, read your newspapers, go to your movie shows, we will be winding in the wind, milk bleeding into the sea all Tarkovsky-style it whispers. From where before they fled and fled prior to that, there isn't much left. The termites, they are subterranean, they ate up the floor and the rest all just gave way like tug of a shoelace during a winter storm.

Kiss
Roger The Janitor

Buckets of confetti
capsules of blood
sweeping the planks of casket salesmen
it is Easter all night
a party for the lower waged earners every day
upside down in the rafters
unseeable in this lime lit hideaway

This room reserved for coarse unbleached take out napkins
packets of blushers drying out in the rain
what they wanted from you, I did too
but at a much different time

a hundred shades of electric blues
inverted chords from radio tunes
here is another one too, that will have to do
the finished version is in the green room crying
arriving late to swim in the airborne ticker tape

in my arms you felt as I imagine a freeway might
were you to hold it whole in an embrace
jutting to the left
searching for escape
seeking only escape

it wasn't you
I know
that lipstick is not your color
and you were never my age

I'm 93 and you remain sixteen
Lon Chaney in kerosene capped teeth
black grease paint, wolf meat wig
cow tongue, store bought rattlesnake jacket boots
kicking
nervously
at the leg of the sofa while being interviewed
there is nothing here to see folks
there is nothing here to hear
I am before you
then backstage
crushed forty watt
uncapped sharpie on a paper plate

PHARAOHS

VOL. 2

I T WAS A SUNDAY, and tickets for the Kiss concert at the Anaheim Convention Center for November 6th, 1979 were going on sale. We asked my Pop if he would take us to see Kiss for the second time, a two bobble head preteens begging, he agreed. Sunday AM and into his used car we hopped down to the Ticketmaster that was in the then-living mall off of Holt and where Indian Hill deadends into Pomona. There was a line, but the line didn't look like Kiss fans (and post solo albums into *Dynasty*, those fans were for the most part all under 16 years old). Bearded, potbellied, Zig-Zag stained shirt flip flop dudes dotted the sidewalk. Feathered roach clips in hand, and certainly-imagined sport coat patched elbows that come courtesy of what would be my Montclair High music teacher who loved Chicago, Steely Dan, and other true rock musicians that could read charts; true rock musicians, hilarious. It had to have been my father that asked one of those boho neo jazzbos if they, too, were in line for Kiss tickets. The schoolmarm response, "The Weather Report," said in such a pedantic and condescending manner that I packed it away with me to keep until I understood it, and then kept it rent free with me until even now. The Weather Report. I imagined them being like Earth, Wind & Fire, whose "Shining Star" was on our radar from *Casey Kasem's Top 40*. A ten-year-old imagines that the elements and the forecast are tied together, so must these two bands.

When I got around to hearing The Weather Report five or six years later it was a huge disappointment. Jazz Fusion, what a fantastic name for a music genre, what could it mean? Fusion of jazz with what? Well, a mindset of a Montclair High music teacher and jazz, is what. True rock musician. It took me years to circle back to Miles Davis after the burn of picking up *Bitches Brew* as a teenager, a record as good as The Who's *Tommy*, Derek & The Dominos *Layla* & anything by Mahogany Rush—to the resell pile with all of 'em. It wasn't until my early twenties that I started to scratch at jazz again, this was the era of great free players like William Parker, Charles Gayle, Matthew Shipp and further outré vets like Arthur Doyle and Wadada Leo Smith et al. Jazz was not yet quite dead. Skip "Pharaoh's Dance" from *Bitches Brew* and fast forward right on over to Chicago's Pharaohs. Jazz Fusion would have been better served as a means to describe The Pharaohs, Maurice White's pre-Earth, Wind & Fire band that released two albums. Take a look at any picture of them and if you were scarred like me, you might get the heebie jeebies, oh no, a dude on the congas, another on two tom toms, on top of a full time drummer? Is this going to be like those early pre-Steve Perry Journey records? Of course not. A finer boat built from the ark of soul and the tenants of jazz does not exist. Their moving cover of "Tracks Of My Tears" sits on the same record as their sprawling jazz original "Great House" which does in fact veer slightly into the Pastorius pantheon, but stays focused to the betterment of the groove. Weather Report's 1978 record that maybe they were still touring out when those Kiss tickets were purchased was *Mr. Gone*, an above par name for a record. It included Jaco's "Punk Jazz," another decent title for a track. But oh, if only. Like other pillars of society mocking youth culture, the track starts out with a bass guitar workout by Jaco as if to show youngsters what "Real music" is before leaning into a farting dental lab pipe in synth led "Funky" jazz blanket. Joe Zawinul and Wayne Shorter, you burned me again, but by my mid-twenties I had found *In a Silent Way* and moved past my resentment.

TONY CONRAD MEETS ARNOLD DREYBLATT

E VEN WHEN A YOUNG PERSON'S DREAMS are
so minimal, and take so little effort to birth, there can still
be such a wealth of clouds obscuring the entryway, naysayers
screaming from their fire escapes, sending out carrier pigeon
hate mail in an attempt to not only sully that dream, but push
that thought back up the canal of thought, back into the creases
of the mind in an attempt to lock those most nominal of visions
away, so that those dreams appear further away and nearly insur-
mountable. When your mother is a painter, and your father has
the funds to ship you off to college, well, those are the brand of
golden tickets that most would punch and use with nothing in
customs to declare en route home. In a vacuum, creating mechanical language, writing code, programming a motherboard with
mercury bubbles soldered onto the memory, black widow eggs,
them spiky sacs silvered over to hatch in a century. We thought
these computers would last a dozen millennia. They were the
first chapter, to be added onto, not discarded with new models.
Younger, faster, quicker, leaner, yer old man's fantasy. Beneath
a linen pillowcase, one tone, one note. Here is something I can
remember eternally that no one can take away. The entirety of
it is in E.

Tony Conrad and Arnold Dreyblatt went to schools that
opposed one another, a Beatles vs. Stones kind of thing; one
couriered off for art school damage, awaiting a welcoming to the
gallery where the other was at war with lions at the door with

their velvet ropes and bouncing clipboards. We were given four chambers and a couple of lobes so we can easily compartmentalize all sorts of things. I work fairly hard to keep the two of these musicians as far apart as I can in my record collection and also within me. We are, all of us, I know, doing what we can for the sake of art. The documentary on Tony Conrad, *Completely In The Present*, offers as many reasons to love him as a person as it does moments when you might want to pull aside the then still living Conrad, and say to him as a pal, "Don't tell them that," "Don't reveal too much," "Don't protest too loudly about what you can't stand, you don't know how these cameras and booms are going to relate that through their hollow-bodied souls." Too late. It is all there. Even the stumbles, though, are great. Maybe you are a fan of outrage, outrage married to comedy, even more so, well, here is your documentary and here is your man in full widescreen frame. Speaking, performing, and sharing his films, when for decades all you really had were some stately moments of him with Faust. There came the reissues of that recording of his with Angus Maclise, La Monte Young, Marian Zazeela and John Cale from 1965 that saw the light of day in 2000 (this following a new recording and a few reissues in the mid '90s hot on the heels of the 1993 reissue of that classic record of his with Faust, *Outside The Dream Syndicate*), but now, here he is, being interviewed, performing live here and there, and ending his life with a cancer battle and this documentary. Here he is, baring so much that us listeners had never heard nor seen, that I nearly asked the projectionist to turn the film off after ten minutes so that I could take it in by the chapter, one ten-minute segment a week through the summer.

Dreyblatt, like Conrad, is not just a composer/musician, but also an artist whose lenticular works blur lines of script with movement. His excited strings can recall the exotica of Martin Denny, the free jazz pump of Archie Shepp, the clustered chords of Charles Ives, and the patience of Phillip Glass. Much like my reference earlier in the book as to how I imagined Billie Holiday sounding more like Ida Cox, who I will take any day over Holiday, Dreyblatt uses much of the same arpeggiated chords that Glass employs, but instead of that vocal harmony running up and down the windpipe at a breakneck speed, here we take it easy, get to know each note of the arpeggio. We land on a chord and kick at its tires, check the odometer, run our finger across the dashboard, amazed at the curve of the world design as it bends to the passenger side. Foot pace, taking it all in, it is a good twenty-two minutes before we realize that it is two of us in the car with his cassette jammed in the deck. This is the music we imagined was built to deliver us. There will not be an exhibition statement next to a plinth with a boom box that plays a fourteen hour loop of Dreyblatt's tunes. It can be heard as high art, but it speaks so easily with the listener that it is understood by any that come in contact with it. These are the blankets that warm your favorite hip hop bed, these are the sounds that lurk around the corner of your dearest films, and here are the unexpected turns that amazed you at both low and high speeds.

Here are two artists, so similar in so many ways that I imagine them absolutely loathing one another gathered over a meal at your freshly painted flat. Quick, open the slider, one needs to smoke and call the other one a prat while the other rolls his eyes and complains. High art comes from a very simple place. True art manages to occupy everyone, even if only momentarily, to whom has ever been displayed. Imagine how difficult it was for these two musicians to find a stage, and then imagine the fight they had to muster to remain, to play, to take all the shoulder shrugging and criticism that certainly came their way. When you begin with nothing, you aren't shocked to end up that way. The lights come up, and holy shit there are fourteen people still remaining in the place, the place that we began. A victory for the patient. A win for every one of them patients that run around our heart and mind, unwiring our waking life in dream.

RED TRANSISTOR
S/T

GUITARIST RUDOLPH GREY was in a triumvirate of incredible bands. He flirted with and briefly joined the New York No Wave band Mars before starting the short-lived Red Transistor in 1977 with VON LMO. Their *Not Bite 7"* got lost in time and was not issued until 1990, an incredible document of an incredible band. With The Blue Humans, Grey achieved what The MC5 sought out to do—marry the ferocity of savage rock with free jazz. A live record of theirs recorded in 1980 gives the listener pause to hear that No Wave guitar of Grey's slammed against them Beaver Harris drums & Arthur Doyle sax. Arthur Doyle could be found early on playing back up in the band, six feet in to the back of the stage, in the darkest corner while Gladys Knights & The Pips sang. Later he would work with jazz greats Pharoah Sanders, Alan Silva, and drummer Sunny Murray. Beaver Harris can be heard on the classic mid to late '60s Archie Shepp records on Impulse as well as side steps with Steve Lacy, Marion Brown and trombonist Roswell Rudd. These are not dilettantes playing necks underwater, this is the real shit. It is worth repeating that this is what MC5 was attempting to do, but here it is done with a focus on outsider jazz instead of jams. This is what I was looking for when I bought *High Time* after *Kick Out The Jams* didn't hit me as hard as I was promised it would when I was a teen. Rudolph Grey's guitar playing? The whole of New York scuzz owes him a big wet kiss. He took the Derek Bailey school out of college and, with Sonny Sharrock and Peter Brötzmann, returned it to a hard-on high school pulse that would later be the skeletal ash for Thurston, Nels Cline, Marc Ribot and countless others to snottily sniff up and build upon.

Those three years in Grey's life are enough for any lifetime, but there is more. Some great records featuring members of Borbetomagus, Coltrane's drummer Rashied Ali among others on the Southern California New Alliance label, a subdivision of SST which is where I came to learn of him at the begin of the '90s. Where is he now? Barely a presence? You'll find talk and tale about his book on Ed Wood, or how his obsession with Wood led to him finding Wood's last film that was long thought lost. Grey in by the fire exit, quickening his escape, he doesn't need a crowd.

OTIS REDDING
OTIS '92

T HE BIG BOPPER'S CALYPSO RECORD. He would
have been late on the wave in 1960, but had he lived, he
and James Moody would be touring together that year, playing
their version of early Soca music. Is that why the powers that be
took down that plane? Everything is up for debate; the facts are
attacked and debased. Our memories are not to be trusted. The
first time I heard Big Bopper's "Chantilly Lace" was in a pet
store in Montclair. It was one of the most frightening moments
of my life. Five years old, some creepy crank call, is this some
kind of joke? Is this even music? What in the hell is going on? I
would not be that frightened again until at the age of seven I saw
Burnt Offerings at the Mission Drive-In, 1976. As if Oliver Reed
drowning his kid wasn't scary enough, the Vaseline close-ups of
Anthony James as the hearse driver scared the dead bejesus out
of me and a bunch of other kids that stumbled onto this film
too early in the day for them to be viewing it. Years later when
I saw James in *Vanishing Point* and *...tick...tick...tick...*, my body
muscles remembered that face and tensed up.

My father, he was the genius taking a seven-year-old to see
Burnt Offerings, he was in that pet store when that god damn
Big Bopper song came on too. Beyond the grave, all of those that
have left us, they roll upon the shore, and they come to us in
waves. We raise our kids, and in the present tense, we are trying
to give them something to gird themselves against the trouble
and the indecency of this world. We hope that they will forgive
all of our shortcomings, many of which will not be apparent to
them for decades, some decades after we have ourselves said so

long and good riddance to this attention deficit curve. We feast on the table scraps of songs like "Ooh Carla, Ooh Otis" from the *King & Queen* record by Carla Thomas & Otis. Carla's father, well, he had songs about chickens and dogs, a comedian talking about rabbits. I come from a lineage of farmers, from a farmer's daughter, one who as a divorcee took her three children to San Diego in the mid '70s, plugging quarters into the vibrating bed and laughing as her children rode that thing endlessly. Mattresses where god only knows these very positions struck by these three children had been struck before, but not innocently.

You have lost so much. I see it everywhere I go. All of the loss, it serves as maybe a starting point or a place to rest your hat—but it needn't. Do you think Otis Redding would want you to do that? Do you think your pals and blood would take comfort in that? Rilke tried to tell you, Oliver Reed shook you to your foundation trying to get your attention, hell; they called in Bette Davis, Karen Black, and from Newark, James Moody with his Bahá'í faith in an attempt to console you. In your bed, curtain drawn, and from the sidewalk, maybe it is only a couple, but it sounds like a choir singing.

Nam-myoho-renge-kyo.

THE WAITRESSES
NEW WAVE HALLOWEEN

ALL THEM CIGARETTES, you were only forty when you died, was it all them cigarettes? Was it the asphalt or the sulfites or red dye number fives? You were born in 1956, just before the birth of swiveling hips and dapper danned hairsprayed men, ten in '66, and a high school graduate in 1974, what a droll time to be a teen. In Cleveland though, there was something bubbling up under that cement during your formative years. Electric Eels, Rocket From The Tombs into Pere Ubu, Mirrors, The Styrenes, Lucky Pierre, Devo. Michigan and New York above you, Kentucky below you, is it any wonder that the Cleveland sound is the sound of sputtering antique technology, whirly bird rusted transmissions that weren't listened to, they were just always there, in the air. You, you have to be heard again, as in, is that something we heard, really? That was the music that was growing up in your neighborhood when you were fourteen and sixteen and eighteen. Were you even aware that it was there, Patty? Was it Utopia and James Gang and Janis Ian and Bubble Puppy that were on your FM while all that noise was in little clubs away from your stretch, in little garages in neighborhoods block after block away from yours?

Patty, as the singer of The Waitresses, yours was a decidedly east coast, once-removed vocal delivery. The not pretty enough for prime time features that I imagine led Debbie Harry from New York, Suzi Quatro from Michigan to be front women could be argued, somewhat lost on you. You were more in line with your southern neighbor from Kentucky, Loretta Lynn. No leather jumpsuit, come hither soft focus frame. Yours was more of a matter of fact smart ass, unafraid relatability. One that makes the two lines that you are most famous for in song so real to the listener. Hard scrabbled, leaving the party alone at 10pm, smoking your insecurities away on the sill of your mom's home, Lysol at the ready. The realities and fantasies that are told orally by family members about their family line are blurred and bloodied with all kinds of omissions, overstated facts and just plain untruths. You cannot trust the narrator, the autobiographer, the hanger-on or the lover. The source, depending on the facts at hand, may have played that memory to death and forgotten the subtleties that made it memorable to begin with.

I know next to nothing about Patty Donahue's life. I have read hundreds of biographies/autobiographies in my life, but some artists don't have a large enough audience or a marked enough life to warrant such a tome. There is a pantheon of artists who have innumerable books written about them that I have steered clear of. I know enough, or want to keep vague enough my anchored facts, to let the art breathe. The screenwriter, the director, the cinematographer, the scorer, even the graphic artist for the movie poster is of more interest to me than any actor is. Same goes for music. If the singer is not also a songwriter in the band, I tend to care less about the singer's story than the keyboardist or tambourine player. This is not to denigrate the talents of Jimmy Scott, Roger Daltrey or Anita O'Day. An important part of the canvas for sure, but the thoughts & musings of Joseph Cotten or Rita Hayworth, as interesting as those might be, don't pull me in like what was going on in Orson Welles' mind during the creation of *Journey Into Fear* or *The Lady From Shanghai*. If actors and singers are simply interpreters, then let them be that blank canvas to me that so many of them have asked to be. No need to guard your privacy from me, just passing through, sir.

An actor takes on a role, a singer's output can be stacked one on top of another, then another, 45s in a jukebox, each one a scene, a vignette, resequenced and edited into whatever form the listener desires, easily. The Waitresses have that kind of attraction for me. I was never a huge fan, but they were in the air, and they were unique. Even now, I am working to keep that canvas blank and not cheat by throwing them into an engine or in a turn of the counter stall. Instead, I suggest, pull out the LP sleeves to read the liner notes. Let's keep this relationship professional. You know next to nothing about me, and me, you. When one of your two hit songs comes on the car radio at Christmas, I'll keep it tuned in and will probably even nudge the volume up a bit. You mean that to me. You are one of us. Gilda Radner, Joey Ramone, the weaker poems that could have been a lost stain in the laundry. Tom Landry, Peyton Manning, them, I could care less about. You, Patty, you was a $10,000 one-time Fay Wray. An agitator, pulling at the top and then the bottom jaw all King Kong style, to make sure we was here, awake, watching your every move.

Sandra Bell

Again

" **I**F I DON'T GET WELL, it's alright, I had my fun. It'd serve me right after kicking up all kinds of hell. It'd be fine after every which way I tired out the nights. All of these dust-covered spines will fade in time, and the binding will, in centuries to come, be thread that weeps as you take it down from the shelf to see what edition it is. Turn the black light on. Turn the day off. Turn the black light on. Turn the afternoon off. Did they really use glue then and bleached pine? I am hoping that if centuries can do that, then a decade will have the ability to turn all of your blues to gray. Aged. Behind you. Should they never go away, I'm sorry, I'm sorry, I'm sorry, I'm sorry, I'm sorry, I'm sorry, I'm sorry, I'm sorry, I'm sorry, I'm sorry. For every last fight, I'm sorry, I'm sorry, I'm sorry, I'm sorry, I'm sorry, I'm sorry, I'm sorry, I'm sorry, I'm sorry, I'm sorry. For this, my first goodnight, there is a limo stretched out before us. I don't think we should do what is expected of us. I think we should bring that death mobile to its flattened curbside knees, praying, within earshot of the church, pleading. Make plain the argument that it can't take you."

"You sure enough have been kind to me, and we had us some fun. You were kind to me, stretching out thin your light, just enough to splash and illuminate the cold around me. I won't, I promise, nightly into the quiet. I will tooth and nail, fight at yours or mine that right at our doorway is calling us. It is calling us, calling us, calling us, calling us, calling us, calling us, calling us, calling us, calling us, calling us."

"I am building up the nerve not to answer. I am, alongside you, building up memory muscle. Recalling what went before. Again."

A voice in the rearview, it is easy to say only one or two things clear and appear calm and collected. My tongue had tripled its size. The corduroy pants had turned to crushed velvet as my bee sting thighs expanded. Dear so and so, hold me in. Don't let me begin. For once I start, I can't stop. Sandra Bell, 1978 David Bowie Marlene Dietrich *Just A Gigolo*. Don't cry, please don't cry. So much of our life was built to be momentary, to make no impression, to be forgotten so that there would be less to house, to move, to throw away at the end. I recall the timbre of your voice then. You were singing and I was mumbling, so surely, you couldn't have made out a word that I said. The photographer said she would meet us at The Grande, on the way to the car we decided instead to be alone at the Motel 6. "This, we will surely remember" you laughed. I laughed too. Laughter spilling out of the cracked window down to the asphalt and yellow powder paint.

THE PILTONES

WHEN THE MOLDY PEACHES first came on the scene, I must have made an unconscious decision to stay away from them. I heard some things here and there, and various friends were trying to get me into or out of their court, but I didn't turn over that rock until years later. Not my style to do such a thing, even now, I am a fairly avid listener, reader, viewer and have always been curious about what is rearing its head under the skin of the mainstream. It would be years later in France with Refrigerator writing songs on the fly with Kimya Dawson and Toby Goodshank, seeing The Piltones live and years later corresponding with Adam Green, all members of The Moldy Peaches when it would all come into focus to me. Not only are all four of them on their own incredible songwriters, but the funniest, and sweetest of people. Who skips out on what will probably be her one and only Oscar invite (the year of *Juno*) to watch, mock and laugh at the proceedings on live TV with her pals in Claremont, California? What kind of songwriters choose comedy and punchlines as a method of getting to the bone of sorrow? None of them write in a They Might Be Giants/Weird Al tableau, and all of them share a penchant for couplets that will tear your heart apart. Go on, look them up with legs walking to your car, parking at a record store, purchasing their records and listening. You don't want your first listen to any of them be on some cold computer whose death will infuriate you in a few years after it suffers from viruses and crashes. The Moldy Peaches were filed under "Lo-Fi," a term that better fits the MP3 and the stream, where everything is interrupted or unjawed/synching incorrectly, buffering. Shit, break up with that thing. You will want to unseal the records or CDs (reread this section in fifteen years when some industry drone mag will be aghast at the rebirth of the CD, youngsters will be pilfering Dad's IKEA medicine cabinet full of the things, searching for that disc by Barbara Manning or Dick Diver). Brian Piltin, of The Moldy Peaches, came to me clean. I had barely heard anything by The Moldy Peaches when I saw his solo act/band The Piltones live. What an overwhelming experience to hear a band on top of their game, performing a set list of songs that were all new to me—and each one, a bona fide classic. "Lone Jane V8," you don't even need to hear the song because the title is perfect all by its lonesome, bringing to mind VU, V3, "Queen Jane Approximately," The Lone Ranger, muscle cars, Bloody Marys, ex-girlfriends. I could wax three more paragraphs on it with ease—and that is just the title of the song. Lyrically, maybe it only touches on one of those aforementioned things. A broken down horse-drawn V8 whose owner's master is her beloved dog Fido. The song, like many of Piltin's best, is conversational and rewards on repeated listening with such a clever and understated natural interplay that is charming in its lack of attempting to impress with songwriting muscles or cleverness; clever without being clever. I won't say another word about the other eight songs on the record; you really need to hear the thing.

His one and only CD, the self-titled *Piltones* paper sleeve CD came out in 2003. Listening to it now, I couldn't place the stripped down production and clean/high-end sheen of the thing in time. 1976 Warren Zevon without Jackson Browne and The Eagles hanging around? 1992 Yo La Tengo *May I Sing With Me?* 1997 Brian McMahon's *An Inch Equals a Thousand Miles?* 2003 Angels Of Light *Everything Is Good Here/Please Come Home?* All of these records that are not of their time.

The CD includes his phone number on the back cover, him, I imagine as a kind of Henry Rollins whose listed phone number in the '80s and '90s led to probably thousands of people over the years calling him to say hello (like I once did in my late teens), asking for advice, looking for attention, crank calls undoubtedly. Living in LA, you'll see Henry at any number of shows you go to. Not shirking or hiding, but never drawing attention to himself either. He ain't a punk rock legend; he is one of those musical saints. Brian, in later years, studied the saints and the bible as a born again. Brian, like Hank, steers clear of the illusion of fame. You have to dig hard to find Brian, but it is worth the dig. Brian and I had a few back-and-forth missives six or eight years ago, but I haven't heard from him since. Every week or so I look at the long laundry list of forthcoming new releases hoping that one will be the second Piltones record. But maybe one is enough. The record is perfect.

SPARKS
ON EARTH

Two brothers from LA
asked Freddie Mercury to quit his band
and join them
for their band will be ten times as big
and it will one day
it will one day

Two guys walk into a bar
and the bar is made of solid gold
and it is cooling at 2000 degrees
walk lightly
don't get stuck in that trap

Bergman & Capra
silent but steady
you don't have to watch closely
to understand where they are going
but surely,
that too would help

Two languages
one you can barely understand
I have glasses and I can read
I can read subtitles
so let me help where I can
pie in face
head in hand
the best thing about LA is its slow moving alluvial band

Santa Ana's
inhale & cave
cave in as you are exhausting
all of this energy
exerted to get you simply somewhere else

You don't have to pay them back
It is not that kind of a band
they are slow release batteries
they are never tiring
they are utilizing everything I love about everything
Sharp record cover
smart lyrical reference
hilarious asides
and the B-sides,
well they are just as great
they don't ask for much in return
but god damn it if they shouldn't

THE FALL
TERRA RIFLE

MARK AT 60. Of course 60. What a perfect age for him to float out on. Him responding, "Six-tay und change-ah." It was Mark at age 48 when he visited Pomona, California with his band The Fall. The Fall, playing on the same street that we had booked hundreds of shows at varying venues on from 1990-2005. There was Munchies, a restaurant with inedible food and a faithful congregation of cockroaches that were sure to scatter when Buzzsaw or Les Thugs or Superchunk or Sebadoh played at the venue. We too, to the other side of Second Street, we moved to The Haven, where Beck, Kimya Dawson and The Babies would be booked by one of us with a band once the health inspector put Munchies out of its misery. Interloping a few years later then across the street to 51 Buckingham where I had booked Comets On Fire at their absolute peak—unrelenting, jaw-dropping modern psych. Somewhere towards the end of that all, The Fall played at the then fairly new venue owned by Southern California promoter Goldenvoice, who were just shedding their nascent local tail when The Glass House opened its doors. Here were The Fall, playing on the same street that was home to a gay bar, antique stores, failing restaurants, and thriving artist dens. The Fall, well, they were on a late career peak at this point. This show was post Brownies in NY, where shit fell apart and a young internet was abuzz about arrests and break ups, and came on the heels of the five-piece losing three members after a much-reported dust up in Arizona.

May 7th, 2006 The Brickhouse Phoenix, AZ.

Some stupid with a banana peel burned the place to the ground.

The set starts with the "Over! Over!" and ends with "Systematic

Abuse" both new songs that wouldn't appear until 2007 on their *Reformation Post TLC* record. Could there be two songs to better bookend a band breaking up right there in front of you on stage? It's true; it is all true, that a member of the opening band threw a banana peel at Mark during The Fall's set, purportedly hitting him in the face. Smith removed his sport coat and followed the pitcher of the peel to the parking lot, the band continuing to play as Mark is off stage. Three fifths of the band (meaning that other than Smith and his keyboard playing paramour) quit after the cut-short set. Elena is heard on a rough recording of the show to say to the crowd "I'm sorry, guys. We're really glad you're here but we can't play here as we've not been respected on stage and people have been violent to us and we don't know what's going to happen." [To audience member] "You were. You were cruel. You all were cruel. He doesn't want to come back on and sort these things," just before leaving the stage.

May 9th, 2006 San Diego House of Blues

What a god-awful mess to be in The Fall and playing a show two days later with a new pick up band in one of the tackiest tourist trap clubs, Dan Aykroyd's House of Blues. Elwood, we needed that chicken wire two nights previous to this when the good old boy threw that god damned banana.

May 11, 2006 The Glass House, Pomona

set list:

Bo Demmick / Pacifying Joint / Midnight in Aspen / Theme from Sparta F.C. / Mountain Energei / Wrong Place, Right Time / What About Us // I Can Hear The Grass Grow / Blindness // Mr. Pharmacist

Smith tosses his sport coat by the lapels with his index finger onto his back, paces the left to right of the stage and delivers a succinct, tight drama-free night of newer Fall tunes. Sure, "Wrong Place, Right Time" from *I Am Kurious Oranj* & their defining

cover of The Other Half's "Mr. Pharmacist" are in the set, but
even their cover of The Move's "I Can Hear The Grass Grow" can
be heard on their *Fall Heads Roll* album along with every other
cut, excepting the ones off of the then-new *Real New Fall Record*
a middle class reach
we ant on ant in a flood akimbo for what is out of reach on the
    skin of the water
all the men in our family died young
got no uncles
no grandfather
we are surrounded by women
women who men
women who men

strike the orchestra and reach the balcony
We can afford to lose the high end
we can afford to lose everything
look, up up,
there is a huge hole in the ceiling

TERRY RILEY/
BEN FROST
SLAVE SHIPS

N O ONE HAS PERFORMED the trick of becoming who they are over time better than Terry Riley. That young man should have always been in an old man's body. The skin was unmarked; the lids did not yet weigh enough as they opened up on the world before him when he first began. Look at him now, a wizened old man. *In C.* Such a beautiful and non-descript, yet aptly titled, name for the musical piece. In sea. Is, see? The first performance of *In C* featured Steve Reich, Pauline Oliveros, Morton Subotnick & Jon Gibson. That isn't like a fantasy dream team come true, it is a truth in this fantasy line up. Imagine your first at bat, Dock Ellis on the mound, Thurman Munson catching, Riverside California's own Dusty Baker in the outfield and at bat, the Babe. You can hear the play of the title as you drift through the thing, like that raft in the apartment swimming pool complex that you float on. Your eyes are closed, ice tea in your hand, you think you are in the deep end, your left heel hits the coping, you open one eye to find you are in the kiddie section of the thing, two feet deep and you felt like you were lost at sea. There is fine art, film and literature so dense that the lesser of it gets caught up under the weight of its own knees to never soar. Forever nailed to a gallery wall needing a description of the artist's intent, is that a misery worse than hanging from a cross until expiring? The crowds are coming in and the vultures are swooping, don't give away all of your hard-earned passwords. Make them think. Make them feel. That is what it is, what I hear when I imagine Terry Riley speaking to me after a performance of his. Transcendent. Not walking on the water, but in the water buoyed, floating, surrounded.

Ben Frost has recorded a number of records over the last decade, a student of Eno (with whom he has collaborated); his is a fairly singular voice in the current ambient landscape where hushed tones are difficult to differentiate from one another. Check out his *Solaris* LP which does not try to untangle the narrative of the Tarkovsky film nor cover Eduard Artemyev's score to the film, but lay before us impressions and other possible angles.

At a performance of Riley's that I took my then eleven-year-old son to in January of 2017, Riley was to improvise pieces on his Steinway grand piano to a screen of Doug Aitken's *Migration* films featuring animals in deserted off-road motels. We arrived early and sat about two feet from the foot of the piano, on the cheap carpeting. For a good portion of the show Riley would look up at the screen before him and then lock into a gaze with my eleven-year-old. Eyes on the keys, eyes on the screen, a glance back to Henry. Eyes up, over to the left, and then back to Henry for 15 seconds. This is only the second show (John Cale being the other, check that previous entry and claim yer no-prize) where I was in the presence of the performer not just glancing, but studying, watching and in this case what felt like playing to Henry. Some kind of coincidence having to do with Riley's collaborative *Church of Anthrax* record with John Cale? I would understand it better if I demanded that my family wear Kiss makeup to any concert we go to that was not a Kiss concert. With that I would undoubtedly understand the staring and the dressing down.

THE PHARCYDE
COLOSSUS

THEY WERE DANCERS FIRST. Their lineage ran from The Dazz Band and Rick James through to Jay Dee who produced *Labcabincalifornia*. As any band or clique of high school teenagers can tell you, it is hard to stay together and stay focused. The Beatles had to bring in Billy Preston as a translator. The Everly Brothers, they disagreed about nearly everything. So how then were The Pharcyde supposed to carry on once Fatlip left the crew? The fat gone, then of course the skinny, with Slimkid3 splitting in 2000. The endless hope never dies, bless its big eyes. Fans endlessly pine, picking up lesser records for a few years, then decades followed by table scraps in oversized box set collections, limited-editions, bootleg unsanctioned blips and burps. The well is always there, even if it houses nothing anymore. Fans need to get close to its wet, to pay respect even after that bucket comes back to them empty repeatedly. We are never sated with this disease of Sisyphean proportions, buying and rebuying the same records again and again for their remastering or their bonus cuts or their limited edition sheen. Those of us stricken with this genetic mishap are trying, and trying again, to get to that virgin listen in a drunken haze or a 5.1 surround.

STERLING MORRISON
PACIFIC BEND

A N INSTRUMENTAL SURF RECORD by Sterling Morrison, *Pacific Bend* would have been gorgeous had it happened. Hell, there isn't much of a discography for Morrison post VU, but he did in fact continue to play music after he left The Velvet Underground. He could be seen playing gigs with The Bizarros from Austin in the '80s and you can hear him on a Luna song, but otherwise it is fairly slim pickings. After his stint in the Velvet Underground, Sterling Morrison became a tugboat captain, and so it does not seem that far-fetched that a man with his knowledge of the maritime ways and fluid guitar playing style could easily do such a thing as record a surf record. I can hear his reinterpretations of "Here She Comes Now" and "I Love You" as lilting surf tunes, his understated style in full blossom, at last, in the spotlight so that it could not be Ringo Starred or Don Cherried. Reed has his real as rain "The Ostrich," where for me, Morrison has the imaginary "Alcove of Loneliness Bay" A-side. The seeds of this book are, after all, about imaginary releases, and this one is the most tangible of the 100 for me, I can practically hear it.

There is a history of surf music that originated from the Inland Empire and neighboring Orange County area. Verne Acree of The Blazers (from Fullerton), The Tornadoes (Redlands), and Johnny Fortune whose "Soul Surfer" is one of the ten best surf cuts ever recorded. Fortune was born in Ohio, but made his way out to California with his family when just barely a teen. He lived in Ontario, California when he was my guitar teacher, earning scratch teaching at Upland Music off of Baseline and Mountain in Upland. I recall leather pants, a receding hairline, a keychain with a 2″x3″ picture of him playing on stage with Barbara Mandrell that hung off of his pant loop when I sat on that folding chair with a cassette I had brought weekly, recorded over & over & over again with a song for him to teach me, maybe something by Accept or The Scorpions or Steeler. I recall one lesson wherein he set aside my shitty white shell Pic 'N' Save dub and persuaded me to learn "Crimson & Clover" by Joan Jett. "Crimson & Clover" is, of course, not a song written by Joan Jett, it was written by Tommy James and Peter Lucia. The song was a hit in 1969, the year I was born, by their band Tommy James & The Shondells. I was not a fan of Joan Jett, but was a fan of The Runaways whose record was picked up in what I imagine was the same heated couple of months by my brother and I as *Too Much Too Soon*, *VU & Nico*, *Raw Power* and other proto-punk records we gleaned from a southbound *Creem* that was still reliving its glory days circa 1984/85. It wasn't until years later that I learned the history of Fortune beyond his Nashville leanings (which is the direction he was starting to veer in when he was my teacher). A purported session with Sam Cooke, sessions with Glen Campbell and of course his surfer sides that I picked up years later and still play in the late eves around the house when the time is right.

"Crimson & Clover," I learned the song, and our band covered it early on as it was one of the few covers we could play. Thank you, Johnny Fortune, for teaching me something I never forgot. *Pacific Bend*, what a record that would have been, there is a silence in the room for exactly thirty-two minutes after I play Fortune's surf sides like "Surfer's Trip" & "Midnight Surf" where this record resides.

JANE BIRKIN
CHEAP JAIL TATTOO

WHY WOULD YOU MAKE CALLS to me out of the blue? Is there something in me you forgot to change? My social security? My middle name? None of that meant nothing to me. You, on the nape of my neck, with your *Entertainment Weekly* grip, your handlers let slip that it was only halfheartedly that you came after me. Which two of the four chambers? Am I pumping or cleaning? Well, that answer was all I needed. I never check messages; the phone is always left at home crying itself awake when you call. Leave some hissing at the tone, I will play it out until the tails slap at the cartridge. Are you gonna hassle over being the first one in? Push against glass, demanding entry? Going to threaten the children at La Bodega with a knife of tin? The strings play to impress one another, hard against the softer parts, spitting at each orifice, thinking that is the traction needed to slip in. Savages with their subscription scriptured services. $10 a week buys them forgiveness; you should see what a few hundred can do. Cutting into the air, and the words just lay stillborn there. Ninety-eight cent kite flash neon green mark down cuz no one wanted our uncoming dreams. I'll play on your team, if it is I that is picked lastly. The one to bag sorrow. Receipt away the nervous systems pulled out and splayed, like, is that upside down or sideway? The word is sideways, sideways, side ways. Side, side, side. I'm the last in, so I don't need to be divided. Where even the sugar packets are faked, splendid, devoid of caloric meaning, I suck 'em all in as they threaten to change my DNA. My make. Well, it was our make, and it was troubled. A rusted undercarriage delivering a decision. A decision made up of mostly mines.

Out of the blackness, you shouldn't pull from us there. Out of the darkness, hey, whose side you on? Matte peach index fingernail paint. Mandible clatter. Legs dislocated in the terminex airport. Give this sinking away liberally, sideways. Half here, half away. You was always blurry in yer blues, we couldn't tell from which side you were shooting and which you were denying.

They will name things after you. Things that will disgust you. Things that you can ill afford, and oh shit, that isn't all. The mark that you will make will be the exact thing that you yourself would take one of them ball-peen hammers to. I know you, and you would never want to hurt no one. But when they take your name, and assign it to such things, well then, you are allowed. In the churching fields, they thank their lord Jesus for all of that muddled scripture that no one can develop correctly. You can't quite see it, and it isn't copyrighted, so let's make it a style all our own. Tip of the hat wisdom on a scratched reel of grain where the interests are protected by the high heeling infamy of invested parties. Am I to Stockholm syndrome? Paul Schrader the demons to death? Forgive my captors nightly as I slip on my razored blade sex. Six hours it takes to not cut at the pressing parts. We are one-trick footnotes at best, otherwise, simply forgotten. The docent at the museum eyes me with suspicion. Don't touch or feel or even put sight on these antiquities. These, owned by realtors, designed by wild-eyed peasants. It's a cliché, I know, but back then you wouldn't let their muddy feet onto your Marlon Island, Maharishi Mahesh Yogi mess, a friend of mine explains. How great the unwashed, to make themselves known in this rag and bone man world of reality. They don't grasp the very thing they are dying from. Do they, everything? So put me down, for 1 Monk, 1 Chambers and 1 Graves. I'll listen to infinity. No judge, no jury will I ever believe, even if they are on my side. No judge, no jury, will I ever believe, because of you. If you believe them once, then they got you by the hair, and knowing what they think, such foul things with their robes and wigs built only to disguise their selves from the storm and danger of children raised the wrong way. Why would they, then, out of the blue, call on me and you, when they have already pieced together a better ending?

ROLLING BLACKOUTS
S/T

R OLLING BLACKOUTS C.F. (the C.F. stands for "Coastal Fever" which I guess was too long a band name when they were threatened with what I imagine was a lawsuit by a band called Rolling Blackouts) are from Melbourne. The band's 2 EPs and a record out thus far on the subpar Sub Pop label are outstanding. The begin is always fun, but these modern day Econolines are still packed with as much stillness and solitude as they ever were. On the road, tired of talking but talking to just stay awake, most bands play idiot bingo games. Which one is this? One or the other, it doesn't matter. If you start nodding, driver, bite into one of them lemons on the dash.

ac/dc/bg's
American Music Club Foot Orchestra
Azusa Plane White Bags
Big Youth of Today
Men At Work Without Dicks
Orange Juice Love Jones

It would go on for hours, and it would never really be funny, but thank god it kept all of them guys and gals on the road alive.

before you

PRINCE
BEFORE YOU

I DON'T EVEN RECOGNIZE what I am. My left hip abrasion, I feel the ache pulse through my satin bells. I'll have to visit the mirror in the dressing room, a rash? Did I fall? Brush up during a sprint from the riser against the head of the amp in the practice room? Nah, don't bother to look. What use would it be now? On that plane, they drew blood from my left arm; it looked so dark trapped in the filament of that vial. That blood doesn't look like mine. Mine is more of a Hammer film orange red paint ball. Mine is cheap and inhuman. I have caught it running cold out of my nose, smeared it on my gentleman's best shirt sleeve. It wasn't much. I could taste it as the pool above my lip gave in, unable to hold the bleed back as I rushed to the omnisex bathroom. It wasn't snot and it wasn't sweat.

Omnisex. You push the door open and it is the same toilet. The same sink. It is misnamed. It is a letdown. It is just more fluid and heat leaving my body; it is worse than useless. It is a waste of time tending to this vessel. I should be doing other things— writing, arriving at photo shoots, recording. Twenty-first century feminine napkins, is that a winky nod joke? Want to serve that with a bayonet up through my cervix to explore where the bleeding is coming from? Diagnose the wounds of this ship?

I carry all sorts of dead end passengers in me. Those sycophantic microscopic lice that I read jumped from my Mother's pubic triangle and onto my newborn forehead, not to anoint, but to make home my eyebrows for the rest of my life. I wonder, if I shave them off and apply an eyeline, will that rid me of them? When they grow back will the mites as well? How long do these remoras remain tied to me? How long do they live? When I die, where do they go? I am to be incinerated, but what if I was buried? Would they make their way through the soggened dirt to new life? Do I only exist for them? It feels that way at 4am and again at 10. One piece of unbuttered toast, a small bowl of popcorn for breakfast, over the tin sink I eat. If sinks came in sizes, this would be a child's portion, my spit down the drain of the thing. In the room slid just off the balcony, up the stairs above is the studio where I keep red vines and drinks for guests. Eat now, but only to keep that host body pumping. We need you.

Am I just a byproduct of all of the books that I read, all the music that filled my head, all of the ones and zeroes that used to be music and film on disc, that are now digital clouds on a screen? I am reflecting constantly. I am broadcasting. I am piecing together grocery lists with specific soundtracks. I am working out in my mind if I should wet my hair all marsupial style and comb with my clawy grab to make myself presentable while comparing sodium content in a store filled with like minds. Like minds that won't spend but a moment on me. Why then do I bother to dress? Is that why I stopped even bothering with that? Years ago, years ago.

The tins of her films were stolen. Her sullen youth came back to her three decades later missing a soundtrack. She had spent those years sandwiched between pining, wondering and waiting. I would have slapped hallelujahs all over the mistakenly sent mail. I would have praised the post and the courier and the stop. dot dot dot. stop. Morse code. I gave my youth away. I didn't want it anyway. I couldn't care for it properly. I am ill-equipped even today so please don't come back to me. Stop.

Do you still walk along the halls of that dormitory with only a towel wrapped tight, knotted just below your rotted core aura? You, I have not forgotten. Your musty cereal box musk, your chew toy phone with its plaque-stained rough edges. I am getting physical. They are measuring in me things that I have no use for.

My blood pressure, my body mass. I am none of that. When I catch sight of myself in the side cabin window reflection, it isn't me I see, because that isn't me. I am eyes. Eye am looking and listening. Eye am not recording properly. How then am I supposed to properly reflect? Abstractions. Abstractly. Even these memories that feel real to me, I know they are gone. I know you aren't 19 anymore, living rent-free in some bird dormer, not knotted, not rotted, if you are even there, you are simply existing.

I feel everything as though it is happening to me as that is the only means to which I know how to digest what is before me. I listen closely. When I overheard a voice say, "It sounds like fireworks," the next sound you heard was my pace and my feet running. There is something up ahead in the distance moving. It is inhuman. Curious? Infinitely. Have I the constitution to move forward? Shake off inertia? The energy to expel? I am a low wage earner these last few years, spending more than I take in. I don't have the kind of insurance needed to cover the ponies if I get it all wrong. I have gotten it all wrong of late. I am in a world of hurt that takes courage in musical heartache. I remember that feeling. I remember then, that exact feeling and am so thankful that coupled with all of the pain, this too is gone.

TOM PETTY & THE HEARTBREAKERS
REVERB

I T'S A SAD STORY. An abusive father, a wife with mental problems, two kids he felt were lost to the weeds as he threw himself deep into his work. A band that was employees, fine employees, arm's length friends. A couple of funerals of those he loved best that he refrained from going to out of fear of turning the proceedings into a circus. There is the story about him returning to Florida, and his aunt tossing a spiral notebook at him, telling him to sign as many times as he could until he got tired. TP declined. The act of refusal is in large part what defines him. How many songs did he write with refusal in just their song titles? "Don't Do Me Like That," "I Won't Back Down," "Don't Come Around Here No More," "I Don't Know What To Say To You," "Stop Draggin' My Heart Around," "Don't Fade On Me." The legend and lore of not settling with Shelter Records, not letting MCA raise the list price on *Hard Promises*.

There was Del Shannon pleading with Petty not to steal his guitarist Howie Epstein away from him, Howie in turn getting messed up on heroin with Carlene Carter and it ultimately costing him his life. Epstein's was one of the funerals that Petty didn't go to. Epstein and Petty's mother, those were the two unattended funerals that get notice. In the throes of his own addiction to heroin, Petty still managed to dig deep into his work. At the tail end of what some call his second hot streak consisting of *Full Moon Fever*, *Into The Great Wide Open*, the first Traveling Wilburys record and *Wildflowers* was the soundtrack to *She's The One*. The record includes The Heartbreakers, Lindsey Buckingham and on the track "Hung Up And Overdue," Carl Wilson of The Beach Boys on vocals and Ringo Starr on drums. A gorgeous song that like so many others of his, has that tossed off, anyone can do that appeal. No offense meant, but what other middle-of-the-road rock 'n' roll singer/songwriter has as much appeal? How many strays is one home expected to take in? Carl Wilson, Ringo Starr, Roy Orbison, Del Shannon, Johnny Cash, Bob Dylan, and even in the end Chris Hillman, the man Petty owed more than all the rest of them put together. They all got championed when they were at their nadir by Petty with him producing or writing or touring or performing with them.

He is forgiven for stealing the line "a rebel without a clue" from The Replacements, whose performance opening for Petty on July 27th 1989 at The Pacific Amphitheatre in Orange County was the least noteworthy of any 'Mats shows I have seen. He is forgiven by almost everyone on the face of the planet because they have a connection or a story or empathy for Petty. There is a fifteen minute snippet of Petty and Garry Shandling having a conversation at Petty's house on the complete Larry Sanders box set. The two of them are quick, riffing and ribbing each other, better than Johnny and McMahon, Conan and Andy, Jimmy and Guillermo. Petty is obviously high, having a good time. That is probably how he is remembered best by his legions of fans. With that wry grin, holding in a punch line that he is too stubborn to share with you. His songs are simple, some deceptively so, and his growing up and going down stories aren't that different from the stories that we have; the stories of our families and our friends.

SARA CARTER
ALONE AT LAST

LODI CALIFORNIA 1980. What an awful place for an ending. There, in some second tier Creedence Clearwater song. The city runs up the pole its claim to fame as the zinfandel capital of the world. You won't find a mention anywhere of their most famous resident, Sara Carter. Her songs and her life may not fit into the script of wine tastings and weddings. Divorce. Surrender. Sure, you pulled in; you picked up my kid, with your hair dye and gaggle of new friends. I know none of them. Them one year kind, they are here and gone, kiss them for me as they will soon to another belong. They are disaster lovers, looking always for the chinks in the armor. Is that what we were arguing over? I lost in a joust, pacing the floorboards until all my powers got leached out my heels and into that low-rent room. I lost myself in some kinda court case. Arise alone, I do every day. You think there is someone else there, up above? Someone peering down with an all-seeing, all-knowing pharmacy filled with endless prescripted vials of endless love? Do they have something I can take to get rid of this heartache? Some sort of Prince/Tom Petty parlour game that I may have that right hand for? Pulling quarters out of my ear for whose sake? Rise alone, sun, lift up all your dead weight, for I am only on fire for you. Forecasts predicted by I Ching/tea leave reigns, well, look here, closely. I'm still the same. My hair is still curly and my eyes are still blue.

Once all that you ever wanted has been turned against you, well, there are no more turns to take. Pull in, pull in, straight. Then, just as quickly, leave. Did Maybelle tell you that? I know we are all gnawing at our ankles trying to get free from this here trap. I tell my best friend again tonight on the phone about where things are at, he says you gotta sink your teeth through the loose flesh and get right down to the bone. I don't, on my own nor with you, want to go there. I don't want to acknowledge this corner that you are in. It is just too awful of a place for me to leave you after the many entry ways to salvation that you afforded me.

THE BANGS
LIVE ON RODNEY ON THE KSPC

THERE ARE SOME DJs that you feel a kinship with fairly immediately and others that take decades to win you over. The glory of local terrestrial radio is that the DJs on-air are attuned (in varying bands) to the community that surrounds them. They may love the scrim foot hippy granola mold, hate the skateboarding ruffians, cut in front of you without signaling, but they are there, breathing the same pollinated air as you. College radio offers the best and worst of this world. Eighteen-year-olds with no musical history and uninformed opinions and eighteen-year-olds with vast musical knowledge for their age and a thirst and passion that even in the deepest dyed music lover wanes and diminishes with time. It is our duty as listeners to be forgiving of the new DJs on them left-of-the-dial stations whose pay rate is invisible and audience unavailable for comment. If I don't like your show, I am not hanging around cheering you on or anything like that, I ain't no helicopter listener, but I'll sit through yer umms and mispronunciations, your shy back announce and stumbling PSAs if you are playing a mix of worthwhile music or some curve-balls between the balls and strikes. There are commercial DJs I have a soft spot here or there for only because they have been part of the fabric of my life for thirty-plus years as I switch around the dial in the car, but a connection? You? There are the awful music shows on the three NPR stations that are in my range, the largest offender being KCRW with their brand of watered-down neo-soul, flaccid electronic fusion, and awful alt-rock. The oldies stations reach to *Rumours* or The Stones for a deep dive, and other than getting a Pusha T track here or a Kid Cudi track there, commercial radio isn't something that offers much to me. The wonder of Southern California is that Pacifica radio is still alive after all of the political infighting and underfunding. Like other left hand bands, some of the greatest radio shows I have ever heard have been there. There is a surplus of fantastic Latin music stations where you can always find a Merengue, Norteno or Banda song on the band worthy of your travels, and between the college radio stations (KUCR, KSPC, KXLU, KUCI), now streaming on yer digital appendage and available as I bounce from county to county, you can still find something on that purportedly dead radio of yours.

Southern California rock mainstays are moving to the digital graveyard, where the signal fades as you duck beneath an underpass or a particularly sticky patch of highway. Rodney Bingenheimer, Jim Ladd, Shotgun Kelly and others made the jump, but again they are soft spots like the scientology building off of Sunset or other haunts you never willingly search out. They just appear on your drive by. How many young artists and bands got their start on our airwaves? One of the few places I am proud that my tax dollars are spent. For our dearth of acting as patrons of the arts in the States, we can at least run this one up the pole beneath your neighbor's "Don't tread on me" flag. Call the wife; remind her to let you know when her husband dies so that we are extra careful to not walk across his grave on our run to the concessions for a death pennant to wrap around our antenna as we drive the Southern California freeways at ten and fifteen mile per hour increments to take in all that they have to offer.

THE UNFORGIVEN
DR. COWBOY

DRESSING UP, ALL SELF-CONSCIOUS and costumed like Generation X, named appropriately and reaching for a grimace à la Stiv Bators but communicating something more akin to King Diamond with his misinformed makeup. There are thousands of 'em. Like a terrible band name or awful cover art, us listeners are so god damn forgiving that I would put most of us up on that saintly rung for this one aspect of our habit. We can forgive poor noms de plume. See through fake biographies. Look past awful graphic art. Even surrender to trite lyrics. Sure, in conversation, we will cut down each other's tastes, hold sacred nothing, get heated over nothing more than opinion, but for this one thing, we will forgive anything if the music speaks to us. Dress up has never been my thing, not in real life, not in my shoddy wardrobe, not in the cars that I drive. I will take my wife fresh out of the shower over makeup and gown any day. That is not to say that there isn't a cadre of this flavor in my record collection. Are you not gonna let Isaac Hayes, Moe Tucker, Rob Tyner, Ryuichi Sakamoto through the door just cuz they spent a bit too much time in the bathroom prior to the photo shoot?

Southern California's love affair with country music is a strange one with its west coast bent that you can hear in all of the artists that spent time being born, raised or schooled here. Merle Haggard's Bakersfield, Lynn Anderson's Fairway and Kris Kristofferson's late teen to early twenties schooling at Pomona College all dot the edges of the records they each put out. Today, you can call Merle Haggard traditional, but when his music arrived newborn, he was an outsider. In came the electric guitar, out went the orchestra. Between him and Buck Owens (We will include Buckaroo guitarist Don Rich in this trinity, as he was as much to credit as the two of them with his unique playbook), they had to create a whole new genre that was named after the city that housed them. Guitar minus orchestra + working class rock 'n' roll pitfalls (sex, drugs, early death) would be found in the next wave of Southern California country tinged artists: J.D. Souther, Jackson Browne, Linda Ronstadt, The Eagles, Poco et al., who all followed a pathway from Gram Parsons. You know that story. He liked to play dress up too, in his nudie suits and semi-forced drawl, would I think him a phony in real time the way I think of The Eagles or the next wave that followed? I think I would see past it, hope I would, in the way I see past the lit set of Iceage or other bands today.

The Maddox Brothers & Rose, they played dress up too. Sure, children of sharecroppers who took the road into California at an early age had some kind of street cred then, and when taken to task for over-accentuating their hillbilly sense of blue humor and over-the-top stage show, any one of the family members could pull that time card from their back pocket. None of it is hard to understand, and all of it is forgivable (to me anyway), when there are performances like "Sally Let Your Bangs Hang Down," "$1000 Wedding" or "Skid Row." From Alabama, Arizona, Florida and other states, many of California's best country artists came. Crawl out of your studio apartment and into your VW. Walk onto the tour bus in your hometown, and exit out of it someone else. Get a quick read then on how you feel about where you left. Was your hometown cruel and mean? Did you need to reinvent yourself, your look, birth date and name, so that they'd barely recognize you when you appeared in the dailies? You got it sort of wrong there, but that is the kind of thing that I love about you. All is forgiven.

MICHAEL NESMITH
THE PRISONER

SWEETHEARTS OF THE RODEO is a fine mile marker for the continuing marriage of rock and country. You can just as easily point to Skip Spence or Townes or Wilco or Dave Alvin as your go-to for different eras of the merging of a fully grown Rock 'n' Roll with its ancestry of hillbilly, bluegrass and western music. Rock 'n' Roll's mother was of course country music and its father gospel. We will only give The Eagles a mention to slight what they did, which was to water down Gram Parsons' cola and add a pinch of butt rock to that mix to make it palatable for the masses. Perhaps they gleaned it from Linda Ronstadt, whose first hit with The Stone Poneys, "Different Drum," was penned by Michael Nesmith. The Monkees aren't my go-to, but I will give them a nod for "Mary, Mary" which is a top drawer pop confection written by Nesmith. Nesmith's talents would shine brighter after The Monkees had run their course with his Pacific Arts self-released records brought to you by the magic of money printed on a liquid paper press. Hal Blaine, Al Casey, James Burton, Buddy Collette, Doug Dillard—a super group that surrounded Nesmith on his early '70s records—make the case that if you have commerce at your back and a give-a-fuck attitude about your audience, well huge small things are possible. It is fitting that Nesmith brought his Texas roots out of the darkness for a series of records that lean towards the honky tonks and abandoned doll huts. It might have been seeing that the back cover shot of *Nevada Fighter* was taken in Indio, CA circa 1970 that led me to pick up that one first some thirty years back at Poo-Bah Records in Pasadena. Indio is one of the cities in the heart of the Inland Empire. The second location of Poo-Bah record store, located in an old craftsman house, felt like what I imagine the Monkees clubhouse was supposed to feel like to viewers. The set dressers were saints, and their selection of records in that tiny house was miraculous.

THE BEAU BRUMMELS
BRADLEY'S BOWTIE

NASHVILLE, 1968. RECORDED just months after The Byrds *Sweethearts Of The Rodeo*, which only hinted at the greatness of what was in store over the next twelve months. The Beau Brummels *Bradley's Barn*, which, each year that I pull their arms out from their sleeves, sounds better and deeper than the year preceding it, followed on the rodeo tail. This call back echo to the previous two decades would not have its rings answered were it not for The Everly Brothers' *Roots* record which served as not only the brothers White Album, but also an appendix to so many artists of the sixties whose vocal harmonies and sound was informed by the brothers. *Roots* is, in itself, the answer record to the brother's fantastic 1958 covers record *Songs Our Daddy Taught Us*. Consisting of covers, excepting the one original by the brothers, "I Wonder If I Care So Much," which in itself is a rereading of the B-side to their "Bye Bye Love" single. The version on *Roots* though, with its sustained feedback and Wrecking Crew drum fills augmented by those distorted and economical Ron Elliott guitar notes, is just as heartbreaking as they bear under lyrics that mean something altogether different now as I listen. Here is the line "I wondered why I had to play" mid-song, enough to break your heart, followed by the coda of "I wonder if I care as much as I did before" segueing into Eliott's own " Ventura Boulevard" making sure that every ember in every chamber is dead, dead out before the song is finally extinguished.

The brothers tried to give the finger to the Acuff-Rose

publishing company which had been dogs at the door post-1964, chewing up the brothers Calliope Records, sniffing out their Dalton Trumbo alias of "Jimmy Howard" by buying up the rights to all of "Howard's" songs, meaning the brothers records from 1965-1968 were comprised of covers. "Adrian Kimberly," a latter 1960's pseudonym of Don's suffered under the weight and worry of legal hassles while Phil's Keestone Family Singers went nowhere, even with Carole King and Glen Campbell on board. *Roots* is one of those Hail Mary passes that touches down and makes certain that the landing will be both fallow to some and serve as hallowed ground for the believers.

Lenny Waronker at Warner Brothers got The Beau Brummels' Ron Elliott to produce and play on the brother's excavation of the past with a spin on the then-present 1968 whose sound is amply heard on the record. Randy Newman's "Illinois" gets the Simon & Garfunkel Tom Wilson jangle; Jimmie Rodgers' "T for Texas" combines the country rock leaning with wah wah nods to psychedelia, and why, there is the more-recent past being dragged into the present with brothers take on former Keestone Family Singer member Glen Campbell's "Less Of Me." "Less Of Me" is treated with a gorgeous production by Elliott and his guitar playing. Eliott's contribution to the record cannot be overstated. "Turn Around," the Ron Elliott co-write that kicks off side one of *Bradley's Barn* loses its foreboding Sal Valentino vocals which pitched the song as more of a warning of possible lost love to the darker of seasons, where in the Everly version, the brothers deliver it with a warmer hue, one that leaves the listener believing that there is in fact hope of the couple rekindling their relationship, of the barefoot girl coming back round the tracks of that train.

Another brotherly duo, the Davies, released their equally nostalgic glimpse into the past with their band The Kinks on *The Village Green Preservation Society*, other family members and recordings of them dating from the previous decade do not dot the corners of the record, but the record has its ghosts. Places and people that are gone, in some cases not yet gone but also not worth rehabilitating to older glory. On *Roots*, there appears the entire Everly family from a 1952 radio recording, the brothers and their parents. Mom appears near the end of the record with a verse from "The Old Rugged Cross" before crossfading into a 1968 cover of Merle Haggard's "Sing Me Back Home" (the interior bookends for the record both written by him, matching the placement of the senior Everly's just before his compositions are taken in hand by the brothers). The past is all over this record, their Ray Price cover of "You Done Me Wrong" is introduced by a sixteen-year flange/delay pedal by their father and "Shady Grove" ends side one with some lo-fi early recordings that might call to mind, in my mind anyway, those early tape recordings of the Fair brothers, or The Barlow siblings (Abby and Lou).

This quartet of records from 1968 were not commercial successes in their day. *Bradley's Barn* would mark the end of The Beau Brummels until a mid '70s reunion (Check Elliott's 1970 solo record *Candlestickmaker*, which is a wonderful little record). *Village Green* is the last record by the original members of The Kinks as it marked Pete Quaife's exit from the band. Gram Parsons left The Byrds not long after *Sweethearts Of The Rodeo* and formed The Flying Burrito Brothers. *Sweethearts* would be his only record with the band. Many have noted that *Roots* was the last classic Everly Brothers album. Define your terms however you would like, there are still a number of interesting side travels ahead for the brothers including the spotty, but nonetheless interesting, comeback record from 1972 *Stories We Could Tell* which includes Don's "I'm Tired Of Singing My Song In Las Vegas." Maybe not meant as an addendum to *Roots*, but it certainly offers a fair explanation of why the past offers itself as the getaway place of choice for so many when the present stalls.

IE FREE MUSIC
SOCIETY
S/T

I T WAS NOT A TRICK. Her silence at the dinner table long after breakfast had been consumed, dishes cleared and the Formica wiped down. The adults talked freely, but she was expressionless, listening only while folding that one-ply paper napkin in and out on that seam, repeatedly, for hours. She couldn't remember any one conversation in particular decades later so much as the action and the act of being in that home, at that table. Gossip and bad politics, meandering shopping lists that took a toll on even the speaker as the droll yawn rolled its way out past them tongues that begged to be wagging. She imagined that speech was created for them in the same manner as oxygen inhaled and exhaled into the lungs, made just to give that organ something to do. Just to keep them pulses pumping, doing something as otherwise it would be a world of nothing. No sound and no movement. Like box elders all gathered around the seed, eating at it in a stateless frozen surrounded circle. Maybe the internal dialog served to strengthen the worlds she slipped into while tedium played out around her. She was ten and then twelve; old needy guests that wouldn't leave even as from room to room in her head she went, dimming the lights. What would happen if Aunt Rose, who like a man dressing for the mirror, missed the whole of her backside, her curled wrinkled blouse folded up the chair back. Her hair extended down from the lobes of her ears to her filthy neck housed in that sweaty pilled-up collar. A side view would reveal what looked like pancake makeup alabaster running up her chin to the marbled dirt caught in her largest wrinkle below her hairline, short Louise Brooks hair on an over-sized canvas. And here she would continue to sit. Microscope dialed in then out by the hands of a toddler, moving too quickly for her to make out anything; the minutest of cells or the near entirety of the thing, eclipsing the slide. "That is what memory does to me," she would tell you over coffee years later. "My heads are filthy, magnetized, I am picking up conversations from every which direction. I can see the filings moving on the table, and I know there is a magnet underneath the cheap pressed board with its horse-glued oak panel, but I cannot get to it."

I imagine you're feeling that you must have then been a rung above a mute, who, over the course of months and years, became a trapping at the table. Conversations deepened, widened over time. Blue language, double entendres, and as the ritual continued, certainly post-puberty, maybe Dad's fear of the sexual undertones ebbed in those gatherings at your house, or his sister's house or at Aunt Rose's. "I am working with ham-fisted tools, trying to get back to tap into it. It is I, Frankenstein operating on a battery instead of a brain, André the Giant performing surgery with hammers and sickles." It is another of those strings of your family's culture that you don't realize are peculiar until your first circle of adult friends forms. An epiphany when you came to find that this didn't happen every Saturday and Sunday in every apart-ment that dotted your block. That as the only child among eight adults, there was no respite for you. There was no one near the vicinity of your age to congregate with, only unspoken rules. No wandering off to read comic books or play video games or watch TV. No staying up late except on Fridays. No sugar, no sale, no weeds pulled from the shared greenbelt, put in a vase as invasive flowers. Captured at the counter, caught in the kitchen, back at that table, building. Most of us spend our youth and early adult-hood wondering who we are or who it is that we will become. It moves from movie stars and scientists to the dread of dead ended, motionless mimes. Middle age hits us, and we wonder where we came from, how we got here. Take swab DNA tests, read family history tea leaves, pre-death bedded questions for the elders in our families. None of it works. None of it works for me. I often find myself on the couch for hours, just the one three-way bulb turned to two, hours in, after a train of thought that bounces along corridors of reality and fantasy, sharp turns or slow motion replays of how better and how best. No one else is here. No one on the fiberglass Bofinger chair, no one at the table like them elder bugs, preying on that one seed, it is just me, solitaire; breathing in to only exhale. All that waste bound in each breath, all that energy used to only expel. Sound. Sound now, I can almost make it out, in the corner, coming directly towards me.

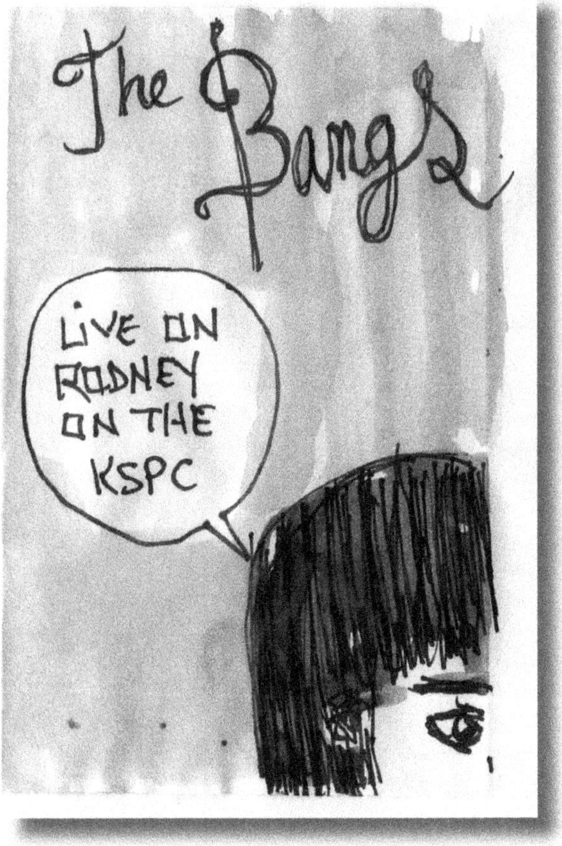
The Bangs
LIVE ON
RODNEY
ON THE
KSPC

THE WE FIVE
PASTORAL POMONA

THE FOLK REVIVAL hit Pomona and the Claremont area with a soft punch in the early to mid-sixties. The We Five's cover of Ian & Sylvia's "You Were On My Mind" made its way up the Billboard charts and into a top five position in 1965. 1966 saw Norma Tanega's "Walkin' My Cat Named Dog" become a top forty hit. The record named after that single has some incredible songs, written by Tanega, as well as a stately cover of "In The Pines" that still holds water today. I dig the wavering vocal that packs emotion where there would now be slight, under pronounced auto tune. The full length record hints at the experimental and off beaten pathways she would go down in the '70s up to present day. There is a reason Yo La Tengo and The Oh Sees have covered her songs, they are both listeners and Tenaga is a voice that never diminishes. Chris Darrow and David Lindley of Kaleidoscope and solo fame both reside in Claremont to this day, Lindley a near recluse writing a letter once a decade to the local *Claremont Courier*, the last one penned complaining about a butcher shop/meatery up the street from his place that forecasted a hive of frat bro drunks littering the street with not only their cheese paper trash, but their very being. What is it that draws us wanderers to stake a claim in the climes that we were raised in? Most of us have traveled all over the country, out of the country. Grew up hating our hometowns or grew old mocking the flavor of them same cities. I looked at Norma's record collection twenty years back, and she was wise to hold onto it. Lindley & Darrow, they dig the roll off of the foothills that is still up for the getting if you are looking north past Bernard Field Station which is one of the few stretches on the main drag where you can grab an unobstructed view of the mountains. Travel around the Inland Empire and the edge of LA that cedes into LA County but that no one considers as such, and the musical history isn't on display. No one is running flag poles or giving home tours of Tom Waits' childhood home or Ray Collins' favorite coffee shops or the stop lights that held captive Patrick John Brayer in the area. You know you are as good as dead when vampires at the chamber of commerce start charades like that. They hated you when you was alive, and they will only be too happy to have never heard of you once you is dead.

STEPMOTHERS
INLAND EMPIRE DEATH SPIRAL

U PLAND JUNIOR HIGH, 1982. One Monday that year, the quad was spray-painted with "SM" logos as were some of the lockers and the basketball court asphalt. I had heard of Stepmothers, but had no yet heard them. That they defaced my oppressive junior high was the highlight of that month for me. I soon thereafter sought out their records. Graffiti works when it is in the right place at the right time. "You Were Never My Age" was the perfect elixir for a thirteen-year-old that needs it boiled down from a meal to a pill. We are terrible judges of character. All the betrayal you see folks hauling in backpacks down the streets given to them from their nearest and dearest. The etched glass work that you hoped someone had broken the pane of so that you wouldn't have to stare at the sad-lined face of the thing at the laundromat nearly every week. That music you hated that you grew to like, that music you loved that you are ashamed of when it plays overhead at a restaurant. There is poetry sewn into our lives. It is sooooo fucking stupid and snide and patronizing, built like most poetry is, like most music is. Can you find it within yourself to love that which you grew out of? Can I find the time to go back, when I am working so hard to push this illusory line of the present to the unknown? I warned you, poetry is in our lives, and it is about time we did something with the 95% of it that embarrasses us.

because now
I am the one
attempting to apply sutures over your yellow kitchen tile
I was a neighbor

we became friends
it was not my will to be in that position
helping to bury your kittens that awful summer morning
scolding your children
collecting your paper when you were away
i didn't want to know what you read
wasn't digging to find your political lean
you came to me
you came to me
from close to nowhere
for next to free
we could never have been fast friends
neither of us would have sought out the other's company
it is not something you would think to seek
our company

there were strangers living on top of us
there were beliefs whose systems were failing
we had to act
we were called on, I believe,
to do something
the sum of these things weighs now heavily on me
as I sit with you, attempting to clean these pulsing stitches
and the two of us can plainly see
not some sarcophagus lying behind us as a history
but a living place in us
these shared memories
that run so deep

in spite of what you became
I love what you once were
and it could be that all of these abrasions and scrapes
well, they were just that
they didn't last
you shook them off and became something greater later in life

let me hope for that
let me imagine that for strangers that make their presence known
   too readily
Coughing in the checkout
Cutting you off before the light
not even signaling
with not even a signal

How much time is left before us
is this needle worth threading?
yeah, I'll thread it for some of you
there are a few saintly things I have done
stumbling with a busted bulb half light
as I graze and scrape against those I love in the ER
galled and bruised
others, I am quite sure,
I won't tend to
and maybe that lack of attention will shepherd them through

TONY ALLEN
UPLAND DISCO BEAT

TONY ALLEN IN UPLAND, in Upland, drumming. That would be like Don Van Vliet in a trailer park in the Mojave Desert, painting. We all have our beginnings, out of our hands how we got here, and a lot of us, endings that will claim us quickly or for others, in such a slow manner that we will end up in the passenger seat of our own lives. The newscaster smiles, "You just can't make this stuff up," awful syntax, weak delivery, fixed teeth. I am just repeating what he said and how he said it. Are there artists today that are developing in a vacuum? A language no one else had ever heard, a technique that took years of isolation to perfect? Years of band aids on them hands, blisters, abrasions, hearing loss, all done in the name of obsession, not in the name of results or commerce or fame. The answer to that one is simple, and no, you can't have it yet as it is still forming from all of them far flung corners for possibly a few more decades. So eat right, get your rest, and take care of yourself.

All those years and all of those records and all of those children born in Africa before Ginger Baker appeared on the scene. Thank god you were fully formed before he arrived at your door. Did he want to have a drum-off? Talk about his inane antics in Ginger Baker's Air Force? Ginger Baker's Air Force, is that a joke? Like Leslie West's compass? Did he think that Paul McCartney was there to steal some creative properties from him too? He had assumed, and you were on to something there even though it was unfounded. Fela walked away after hearing a demo of "Mamunia"; he wasn't after your sound and hopefully nothing else.

Tony Allen ending up a cartoon in a band founded by a Brit

pop poster boy model? Why then, couldn't he have recorded a record live to one track on a handheld Zoom, across from Upland High School in the strip mall that housed the perfect place for a gathering of those in the know to come and see you? The arcade, James Games, there is a PA and a Pearl drum set abandon in the corner, Zildjian cymbals. Zildjian symbols. An ice cream/coffee place around the bend and a chain supermarket just a few doors from there. We can get some gin and bourbon and wine, bottom of the line plastic cups, we could have a real good time. There were precedents. From Japan, Zeni Geva playing in a strip mall off of Bonita and San Dimas Blvd. just five miles away. Weird shit happens here, you just can't make it up.

KORLA PANDIT
FUCK OFF RIVERSIDE

RELATABLE IN NON-EXOTIC FASHIONS, Korla Pandit was not a French-Indian from New Delhi, but a Midwestern African American who followed his sisters to the West Coast for opportunity. Like Gene Vincent, Gene Simmons, Lorna Doom or MF Doom before him, he chose to reinvent himself both physically and in name. John Redd (what a great punk rock nom de plume that would have made) went under the working name of "Juan Rolando" to gain entry into the racist musicians union prior to becoming Korla Pandit. KMPC, KTLA, Hollywood nightclubs, stints as a guest on a myriad of early TV shows and a string of records featuring him at the organ offer suggestions of the talent and soul that lurked beneath the makeup and costume. The issue of race haunts both sides of John Redd's life, for the infliction that it had on his ability to perform as a musician due to his race and for the caricature that he became as a "French-Indian." Passing, and in his passing is when the revelations came out about his private life; his real name, his real race, his moving to Canada with his wife and children to keep their children from being drafted into the Vietnam War. It is natural for youth to be suspect and to be critical. To overreact and to react when for the octogenarian there is no reaction at all. We need pushes and pulls from those around us so that third and fourth looks are taken, so that nothing is labeled, walked away from and never touched again. It is a two-way walkie talkie, and we need to keep all of our thumbs off of the "send" a bit more. This is a toast to all of those that followed after John Redd, who remade their past in an attempt to open their futures and then, miraculously, they did just that.

ALBERT AYLER

HELLS

THERE WAS, OF COURSE, NO JUKEBOX. There were not any chains or padlocks, shackling his body to that thing then thrown into some east-flowing river in New York. Of course, that river would flow east, the one that you were in fact found in. The Western world couldn't make out the shape of your curls, could barely understand the Sunny Murray marching band bleat. The rumor about the mafia tethering him to that thing, well that was just a rumor, a rumor born after long summer walks in Central Park in heavy winter clothes. One of your saxophones chainsawing an apartment TV. You would get down on your palms and knees, psalms to the fata morgana heat, thank you Lord Jesus for all this muddled scripture that as an instrument you have given to only me. To only me to interpret. To give to me to attempt to develop. They are before me; they are me, a great unwashed, Buddy Riching any strides that might be made, because these strides aren't the same. This is a whole different ball game, and here I am, alone in the ninth inning, praying.

A tip of the hat to Winston Churchill, to a black and white scratched reel of grain, where all of the interests were protected, the interests of the moneyed and invested, those that would high heel you to infamy. Am I to Stockholm syndrome? Forgive my captors nightly? As I slip on my razor blade pieces - six hours, give or take, it'll cost me to not cut at the pressing parts, and the most important jig sawed pieces you think you'll need. We are one. Not footnotes at best, at worst, simply forgotten. Why be blue? Is that the saddest of ends for you? Milk carton, anon graveyard burial. Would you prefer, the docent at the museum whose eyes are suspect, to watch over you? Don't touch or feel or even put sight on these antiquities owned by realtors. These shapeshifting designs created by wild eyed peasants, yes, we know that they too are capable of desire & spite & flight. It's a cliché, I know, but back then you wouldn't let their muddy feet onto your isle. Now single file, headphoned, in their own wayward world of false history and fatal mysteries where these kinds of tourists only visit, never land.

Out in the garden, on a smoke break where the interred face up to the granite and crab grass, digitaria for the unwashed. What a gorgeous ending that name has, digitaria. The home for your most paranoid of Mahayana Buddhist leanings, every illusion, properly cataloged and named and haired. The docent, she crushes the Pall Mall on the toe of her high heel, says most of these morons, they prefer the first take. They look at me crazy eyed with all of these cigarette holes on the top side of my Alexander McQueens. The solo instrumental pieces over the symphonies, she continues, they don't grasp everything. So put me down, 1 Monk, 1 Cherry and 1 Ayler. I'll listen ad infinitum. Add for me, infinity. No judge, no jury will I ever believe, even if they are on my side. Believe them once, well, they got you by a hair and you know what they think of such foul things. With their robes and wigs, built to disguise themselves from God, from the *Sturm und Drang*, the Able and Cain, the real things that they somehow have a key to separate; the chaff from the wheat, the bone from the meat, the you from me. No judge, no jury, will I ever believe, because of you. There were no chains. There was no jukebox, just a simple misunderstanding, some misplaced empathy. Dearest of loves, come back to me with your ghosts and your hells and your afterlife tinnitus rings. I will answer, but please forgive me, if my trues and falses fall wrong. I am forever trying.

THE TERMINALS
AM STATIC

OUR LIVES BECAME a mathematical equation. A sell off. Traded in spare time for kids. Kids who grew up on hot sets of boarded up homes, celery cigarettes, and spring-loaded amputee feet. They did then though grow, and they all left home, and once again alone sits this house. A cardboard radio, faucets without plumbing. I don't recognize that lamp, or this Fiestaware saucer; not the green twistee ties next to the sandwich bags. Were they here for long? Something you brought in? These, and the other belongings around here that don't look like they are yours or mine.

Sure, we willingly gave up this and that for health, became risk-averse as middle-aged long passed welterweight. Fifty north of there and counting. I want to see how little we will need, what more we can do without, how long we can go in this hollowed-out trunk of a boat. Well, not so much a boat then, as a canoe.

We watch the tourists down by the seaside laugh up our spills, floating for a minute before being upended. We are a rare treat that only a minor sliver of the population find comedy in. Like them loops of *Guyana's Funniest Home Videos*, truly disturbing to all but their kind.

Our bodies are on fire and we are frantically trying to figure out which parts of it to employ in an attempt to save ourselves, one another. Will I need to walk? Will I? Do I need my left arm? Can I get by without one kidney? Strange thoughts married to strange happenings in the midsection of nowhere. That awful America song, "Horse With No Name," stuck in my head. We are trying to remember one act plays, cheap things to recite to keep one another from truly being here. That is how bonds are formed. This is how bands are born. In desperation, with a prayer. It is usually less than a decade later before they all disband. Reformation blues, minus the drummer or the dead bassist. I don't remember if I liked you, the keyboardist tells the tambourine player's husband. Ah well, think about it over the next decade, you'll need that entry in your memoir. I listen now only to deductions, simple things, an A minor and a G chord. The ending where the ending should be, and the begin; I don't have time for the beginnings anymore.

NICK CAVE
NO SKELETON TREE

If I don't get well
It's alright
I had my fun
It'd serve me right
After kicking up all kinds of hell
It'd be fine after every which way I tired out the nights
All of our colors will in turn fade
turned out blues to an empty gaze
there is no poetry
and there is nothing on
and so I sit in this chair
or in bed I lie
every day
every day

in three centuries they won't be able to discern the pain
the pain of losing one so young
but I suspect that even then
the crowd gathering at the guard rails won't disperse
won't simply go home
they will brave the weather
and they will the dawn
were it I
In their shoes
I'm afraid I would be long gone
I would be long gone
I'm sorry
I'm sorry

I'm sorry
I'm sorry
I'm sorry
I'm sorry
I'm sorry
I'm sorry
I'm sorry
I'm sorry
for this, my first goodnight.

There is a limo
stretched out before me
I think I'll do what is expected
so few options & so little energy
so go ahead and call in the address I am at
call it in
for what it is you think I need
bring me that death mobile
and I will
to the best of my ability
bring it to its knees
to its knees
you will take us no more
to any of your shores
any of your tourist trap luaus
three for five bootleg shirt matinee screens
take us no more
do that for me
and I swear
I will tip generously as you sure have over these years,
been kind to me

We had us some fun
you were kind to me
stretching out thin your light

in an attempt to illuminate everything
I was blind
I could not see
I wretched & writhed
pills and VD
so young
and so dumb
and so lucky

I will tooth and nail
fight at the quiet
yours or mine,
they are still mine or yours
at our doorway
calling us
calling us
calling us
calling us
calling us
calling us
calling us
calling us
calling us
calling us

times ten

LITTLE RICHARD
THE JOE MEEK SESSIONS

THEY ALL MOSTLY GOT LOST in the flood of 1964, but there were some paths out. Chuck had his 1972 record *London* that featured a pick-up band made up of members of The Faces, Van Der Graaf Generator and The Average White Band, Elvis had his '68 Comeback, Roy Orbison got his later in life, but far more interesting are those lost Orbison years and the possibility of what could have been in the sixties through the seventies had these artists been given the space to stretch out if pop music had been looked at as something more than jukebox throwaways. You can hear a touch of this in the single by Orbison, "Southbound Jericho Parkway." It was produced by the members of Neon Philharmonic in 1969. With its nods to "A Day In The Life" and "MacArthur Park," in both its scope and open-ended lyrics married to some soft psych guitar, sitar and Tom Wilsonesque production, it is a found masterpiece. Producers were relegated to the side stages, with maybe a George Martin here or a producer that was given credit for finding new talent there, not so much engaged in the act of recording/producing music with an ear for possibility. Thunderclap Newman, Gary Wright, "Undercover Angel," "Dragging The Line," they were all big zeroes.

No one then would give the Big O the time or the attention that he deserved. A burnt down house, a family surrendered, but still he went on beyond the hot lava flows. Little Richard, he speaks in a deep low baritone when he isn't on *Match Game '76*, *Press Your Luck '80* or Christmas specials. It is no wonder his back ached and he could barely move. What with wearing them wigs and them jewels to just catch your attention while back to the church he did sing. Fair weathered, unforgiving crowds were then searching the inner nets of their souls, self-help medicating to a Phil Donahue, Mommy and me Marlo Thomas pink vinyl line. We were waiting then for Screaming Lord Sutch to wake him from his coffined interior life, waiting for Willie Mitchell to appear for a comeback record production credit. Still in the stands with popcorn and oversized ten dollar programs for a bell bottomed Glyn Johns to offer his RV of equipment to record the man's vocals bouncing off of smoke veined mirrors.

It never happened, and it needn't happen. We music freaks need to move past our wanton desires and selfish needs, forever looking for the best sounding pressing, forever unsatisfied. When we die there will only be a catalog of our spending, our families left with useless walls of musical endings, not sure what to do with all of this obsessive behavior, they will gather it all under tarps in the backyard just to get it out of the house to make room for exercise equipment. No one is waxing poetic on the exhaustive memory of the world's largest Little Richard fan. You are alone for the most part with your passions and your obsessions, unable to communicate to most everyone you come in contact with what it is exactly that you do in your free time. It is better that way, yours is such a great love that it should be a secret world barred from entry of everybody, everybody excepting you.

JONI MITCHELL
MODIGLIANI

THE SUBJECTS ARE LOST, their secrets not worth repeating, my carpenter's a boss who never stops yammering about another world in another time. Another time, another loss.

I can't understand. Guess that's why there are so many courses for the scriptless and the scared shitless who busy themselves needing assurance. The wounded, then the weeping, collecting insurance. There ought to have been a law, she laughs and says, no, there ought to have been a sequel; *Jesus Christ Underdog Too.* It would star Charlie Mingus and Joni Mitchell. The two of them recording a record about their wheelchair bound polio selves in relation to one another. Sue, she is buying up all the black-faced *Don Juan* bootlegs, hearing on good authority from Gail Zappa that this is how you are supposed to do these kinds of things.

She runs to Newport Beach, sitting on a semblance of an architect's idea of a cyclone. The building is moving on tracks, track housing. Clap track meddling, teaching even the seals to read. Cheap plastic sandals melting into the asphalt, feeding the seagulls just outside of the hospital lobby. Thank god there was a pier just steps from the admitting room. Cornering the quarterless, she knows that she herself could have been homeless and that even that could have been ideal. The horizon and its folded-in sun, fucking up the surf, pointing, snickering, laughing at everyone. Some kind of 1972 best old lady in a shitty zine she will be. Hey Joni, put it all behind you.

I could have ended it there, could have crossed myself from a shorthanded list with two fingers in holy water and just three stops missed to attain some form of Santa Monica salvation. After the two of you recorded all the appeals from the artists and their knee filled heels you then had to talk to roadies warning that the throw rug on stage isn't large enough for the backup singers. Don't you get it? They're going to sing up Christmas, going to redress Easter, going to shoot an electronic piece of mail to the publisher. You'd think it was a nation of the state address, you'd think it was something for the people who were prosecuted in parked cars for not speeding along, given tickets on a west coast autobahn for catching breath. The exhales deleted to make room for the future, a future that had we known then it would take the form of a senator drunk on appeals, we'd be sighing still.

Time I addressed these stamps littering my letters in a throw rag bag at the Holiday Inn, time to throw out that lamp high on midnight oil. I have other things to write about she sings. I wish I was and the wish was that I was a million miles from today. Their secrets are sold, so old and out of date, that they are now out of reach—priceless. Time I finally do these things that my friends and I say we will do, before we too, are priced out of the ballpark. Hawking our wares on the off ramps; citrus and roses— shiftless and idle. When will the devil make use of my two red hands? White out them eyes, Cedars-Sinai style. In that waiting room, we all fell asleep, the four of us, on the floor. The helipad is warmed up but we were then unaware. It would be a number of months until we would begin to understand these things that waited for us to only awaken.

JOHN JACOB NILES
NOBLE RED BALLOONS

MARLENE DIETRICH'S PERFORMANCE of "Go Away From My Window" fading into the first line of Dylan's nod to John Jacob Niles' song on "It Ain't Me Babe" fades in and over Patty Waters' raging and ravenous take on "Black is the Color of My True Love's Hair." It will loop and play once more before drawing a breath from the curtains and bringing up the house light dimmer ever so slowly to a version of the song "Black is the Color of My True Love's Hair" by Niles from his *Sings American Folk Songs* recorded in 1941. All three of the touchstones in our loop found a rich place to jump from the unguarded sill of Niles. John Jacob Niles' voice is remarkable, savage and feminine in a vein that Tim Buckley would update years later, and after that Antony & The Johnsons.

Check out Niles' 1952 version of "Black is the Color of My True Love's Hair" on the revelatory *Boone-Tolliver Recordings* issued in 2012 on the L.M. Dupli-cation label. These were live-to-one track home recordings that are shorn of the studio sheen that dots his other recordings. Where he struggles to hit highs, there is humanity and a sweetness that isn't as plentiful on his proper records, but here, on this set, all is revealed. You are welcomed in with a version of "I'm Goin' Away" that reveals just why Nina Simone was so in love with his voice. It is hard to divorce her from him as this plays, as if her vocal is cutting in here and there where there may have been dropouts in the original recording. The piousness and warmed-over Weaver recordings that opened the folk revival house door hold nary a candle to the readings that Niles gave many of those same songs years before. None of the marriage to the word and strict enunciation that ties those readings to rebar, see long lanky hands moving like a theremin over his vocal chords when he sings, releasing the strings, unknotting the tether. On these recordings, he was pulling sounds out of him that maybe even he was shocked to deliver. Like when you nod off with your head pasted to your neck by just a thin layer of sweat, that snore or quick start wakes you with a shock. His was a delivery that scares the hell out of me, makes me believe in them Louvin Brothers end-of-the-world songs, the beg of a true believer to get that upstairs nest ready.

SPACEMEN 3
OCCURRING

C UBA L. AND EVA SMITH, they lived in Bishop California. I know because I have a cancelled check of theirs taped to the back of that Watterson radio that I bought at a thrift store some twenty years back. The check is dated September 9, 1980. What were those of us that were living doing then? On the cusp of a Reagan presidency, I recall my fifth grade teacher, he was French, joking about Dolly Parton. In that class, teaching sex education from his own personal exploits. The '70s had just ended, but the hangover lingered. We had another shared teacher in the room next door. The technology of the day allowed by remote control, a wall to fold in on itself concertina-style to the adjoining classroom and bridge whole the division in our class. There was the viewing of a documentary on the late sixties, assassinations, Vietnam, Woodstock, blah blah blah. The bit about Woodstock stays with me still. Something in me knew it was wrong, my eleven-year-old mind couldn't put it together, and maybe the punk rock conversations or articles in *Creem* had trickled into my consciousness, painted a slant on this. Helicopters flying overhead to show an oversized crowd, this meeting of art and commerce, this seed of mega and super, of Supertrampton, and Fleetwood Mick. Proletariat slim down where choice isn't needed so much.

The present is kicked and bullied, the arguments about the only blockbuster films of the day being based on old ideas. Flipping that tail to whine that there aren't any bands or artists that matter on the large scale anymore. That the 21st century hasn't given us a Beatles or an Elton John or a Michael Jackson or even a Talking Heads; good, I can revisit those old ideas anywhere at any time, their ubiquitous wail and grind in the ghost malls, hold lines and recently discovered physical repacks. I tell baby-faced eleven-year-olds that we have won. That we have kicked down the gatekeepers, that there are endless bands and endless choices and it is damn near your duty, to suss them out yourself on an unending and each day fairer playing field. Anyone can write a song, and now anyone can have that song heard.

Open that door back up on the past by remote control. Show us the 1981 inauguration. And the hostages were just freed. And the hostages were just freed. Take a close look at them presidents, what did they do after their term was served? Ah, Jimmy Carter, you were too innocent and forthright. There was no room for you then, let alone now. There will be forever divisions. There will be divides that we cannot meet Twains in. There, in our DNA strands, you can see them cells circumspective of one another. Sniffing up the waste. I would hope these little beings within us would stop doing things this way at some later date, or hell, they could even start now with me. The dearest of friends, knowing each other's weaker plexus, well, they will upper cut and lower land punches in the heat of divorce so why not then at conception and at birth and up through death. Everything back there is for sale. Everything is still up for grabs. You can see how things get redefined in your lifetime. You can thrift store up the past like that Watterson that sits atop my father's Baldwin piano, the one that our two sons banged upon through their teens.

Would the two of you be interested in each writing your side, writing your side and sending it out to the world? A final proclamation. For all of the unfucked children of the world, I give you Spacemen 3's *Recurring*. Open sesame. With your vibrant kindergarten wrapping, we all anticipated some kind of punch drunk wedding. Another grievance-filled divorce. Another legalese eagle-eyed hurt of the first order. I will get you where you sleep. I will title my songs after places where we have been. I feel so sad sometimes, hypnotized, set me free. I've got the key. I love you, sometimes, hypnotized, reprise. Everybody I know can be found here. And most markedly, I love you. I love you. When we part, and we will all part, how great would it be to say, and to mean, I love you instead of what it is that we have all said. How unbelievable to call on our better intentions. Well, then we could all be Spacemen 3. This could be the final record of our sacrament; you on one side, me on the other. Will I be strong enough to be older brother? Just to see you smile. Just to see you smile again. I love you. Will I be able to vocalize it? Everybody I know can be found here. Will I be able to do such things? Uncoil without venom? Stretch myself so paper thin that even the cheap sunlight will be let in? I have tried. I am trying. Recurring.

JACKIE MITTOO
SUPER CHARGE

IT WASN'T LIKE ACID HOUSE or skiffle or glam, musical genres that are a bit more nebulous and elusive to tie to a hard definition; nor was it like disco or psychedelia, where within a year or two of being birthed, it was already dead. You could see the build with ska, and Jackie Mittoo had a heavy hand in that arc with his Skatalites. This stretched as he landed squarely in reggae circles as a musical director at Studio One where his organ playing has been on some of the greatest songs ("Taste of Soul," "Ghetto Organ") to have been recorded in that studio. In the late '60s up through the late '70s nearly every classic rocker had to take a shot at a reggae song. (Is there a faux reggae song worse than Elton John's "Jamaica Jerk-Off"?) From Clapton, The Stones, Dylan, The Beatles "Ob-La-Di, Ob-La-Da," anything by The Police, it is just a mess of awful on nearly every count. Diminishing returns on these weak winnings would leak like acidic old D batteries into the '80s followed by the even worse 311, Sublime, Dirty Heads yuck of even later on in the eve. Draw up your list of rock/pop reggae crossovers that worked then walk away and let's compare notes.

I wrote down but three successful entries in this crossover that come to mind for me. I'll give you "The Tide Is High" as a success, not one I return to, but I am willing to meet you halfway on that one, so please, all seven of you, don't flood my local post office with protestations and hate mail. The not-that-odd-for-the-time collaboration of Sly & Robbie with Bob Dylan on his *Infidels* record is at number two in this short list. Granted, they are surrounded by the bourgeoisie of rock royalty with a member of the Stones on guitar, Mark Knopfler of Dire Straits at the production helm and his bandmate on the keyboards, but this ungodly mix still manages to make "Jokerman" and "I and I," both with their reggae lilts, successful. Granted, neither of these songs' musical lineage jumps out immediately as being birthed from that genre, but therein is why I think that they succeed. Sly & Robbie's bass and drum punch (even with the unfortunately overly-saturated snare echo) is distinctive and offers the nod as to what is going on here if you are listening.

The unlikeliest of successes in this realm is Pere Ubu's "Heaven" from 1977, the flip of "The Modern Dance" seven-inch single. This is one of the poppiest avenues that train Pere Ubu would ride until their late 1980's run on the Fontana label. "Heaven" is a collision course of reggae down stroke on the offbeat and the grinding coils of Cleveland that bubble up as an alien clarion call throughout the song. "Heaven" is one of those perfect confections that is equal parts candy and meat. Tom Herman's backing vocal gives an emotional lift to the song, sugaring up David Thomas' idiosyncratic vocals that might be too much for the listening world at large. The song, which when substituted for the song "In Heaven" by David Lynch and Peter Ivers that closes *Eraserhead*, works as well as Pink Floyd does to Oz. *Eraserhead* was released less than six months prior to this singles release and even if that film it is not an influence on the song, the two are cut from the same cloth coming to us wrapped in sci-fi noir, both pushing around the soft edges of this newly-birthed "thing," lining their version of dream with an industrial landscape that is haunted by the whirring machines and inhumanity of living beings. If they were both younger, the film maker and the band would breathlessly run home and, as they crossed the threshold of the front door, cry out, "There is something in all of them abandoned buildings that is alive, but we don't know how to take care of it."

IRON MAIDEN
PROUST

BOOK REPORT ROCK. Cliffs Notes for the heavy listener that doesn't have much time to read. Many have argued back and forth that Iron Maiden was not the greatest heavy metal band. I don't believe that I have the power of persuasion to lead you one way or the other, but I do think that it can be agreed upon fairly quickly that Iron Maiden were the best book report band to ever walk the land. Better than The Fall and The Police (who both had a thing for Nabokov). Better than Lou's retelling of "The Raven" or any other in the line I have heard is Iron Maiden. Better than Iris Dement's setting to music Anna Akhmatova's poems, which—though I love it—doesn't count, as there is no reportage there. Let me just scratch the surface with but a modicum of examples from the Iron Maiden canon that they have dissected in song in the event that you are not a listener of theirs; "Ides of March" (Shakespeare), "Murders In The Rue Morgue" (Poe), "Genghis Khan" (sure to help any hessian out when discussing the Khan empire)… and I have another dozen ready at the till to slap on the counter. I am not including other book reports that the band turned in on other subjects ("The Prisoner" enlightened us Americans to the cult sixties Brit TV show, "Quest For Fire" about the film as was "Phantom Of The Opera," " Flight of Icarus" boiled down from Greek mythology with a twist on the father/son relationship not on the original (so be careful there Cliffs Noters).

Samuel Taylor Coleridge's poem "Rime of The Ancient Mariner" is undoubtedly the crown jewel in the many rock 'n' roll book reportages created by Maiden. It is given a vocal workout by

Bruce Dickinson (whose more animated, less street-sounding snarl than that of original singer Paul Di'Anno, adds to the dramatics). Where The Roots or Joni Mitchell might reference a novel in song, Iron Maiden is going to take you through as much of the story and the atmospherics of the thing as they can in three to thirteen and a half minutes and with "Rime" riding that line to 13:30, the dread and the hopelessness of the original is employed not only lyrically, but by wah wah bars to call in the undulating undrinkable sea, tempo changes as weather patterns and economical riffing where the bare minimum is needed to move the story along. Bruce Dickinson is so invested as the narrator of bassist Steve Harris's lyrics (in most cases) in these reports, that the bombast coupled with the naïve greenery behind the ears would be hard-pressed to hold its weight by most bands. Most of the recordings I referenced above were recorded before or on the cusp of irony and arm's length cool invading the music scene. Maiden's lyrical content didn't move into that arena during that era or anywhere else after that period. I'll accept acting and role playing by Dickinson as a method to further underline the point of these reports, as they are oral reports after all. I find that I can't help but root for him regardless of the mettle of the man he is portraying, just as I find myself doing when watching turns by Vincent Price, be they heroic or heinous. The dude is in character, as much as King Diamond or Ross the Boss of Manowar is in character, except he is not only trying to get you to bang thy head, but to possibly use it.

BIZ MARKIE
SHIT BURGER

WE HEARD **BERNARD PURDIE**, John Bonham, Clyde Stubblefield, John "Stabo" Starks, Ziggy Modeliste, Benny Benjamin—all on the drums, beating the hell out of the present to bring forth the future. For some it starts with the bass drum, then the hi-hat, the snare and the toms, plural, cuz you need two of them things. Economically. You only have two plays, so you have to be mindful, as to lay down them two things. There had to be quiet, silence, otherwise there was no relief. Had you not heard "Hot Pants"—Momma come here quick, and give me that licking stick, maybe you'd think twice about voicing what you had penned, Biz. With that Freddie Scott bed behind him on "Just a Friend" and his schoolboy shrug, Markie put together one of the most succinct, heartfelt, truest love songs ever written. The Fat Boys and other comedic hip hop (No, Mario Van Peebles in *Rappin'* does not count) has its place, but the pathos and outside in the rain, tucked inside at a sill hamburger chomping put-downs have never been as ill as Markie's. My chin in the arch of my cupped hand resting on a desk, daydreaming about things that nearly drive me cross town to see your therapist. What the hell am I doing, thinking about this? I have bills to pay, a tree that isn't going to burn itself down. But still I am drawn in, past the butterfly forest of ice cream-scalped diabetic feet, the sun and moon and scars, there is another land. In that land there is no side stage, there is just one stage, one PA and no MC. I am thinking about the kind of bills that Biz would have put together, laying all of them walking oil slick promoters out in a hay field of shame. "Out of business you all go," I imagine Biz saying on a rotary, slamming it down with cigar in hand. His Bizfest would slay music lovers. Isn't he just the kind of fellow to have booked Orleans to follow Carla Thomas, and then bring out Donovan and Shirley Collins for a shared set? Nu Shooz, Kraftwerk, Nat Adderley and Angel Corpus Christi follow. So then who is going to follow that? You would never know, as it would all be kept as hush hush as possible. Mike & The Mechanics, shit, I hate Mike & The Mechanics, but I hear that Lyn Collins is waiting in the wings. Unexpected, refreshing, that is why we still play our Biz Markie records in the twenty-first century.

JERRY LEWIS
SINGS EVEN MORE +
MORE + MORE

WHAT A BRILLIANT FINAL JOKE on us did Jerry Lewis play. He spent four decades begging us not to Brer Rabbit him into the briar patch. His *The Day The Clown Died* has shown itself over the last few years. You can find a forty minute cut of it online (well, if the clouds are around, and your low-rent antenna is up). It has a decidedly foreign film flavor to it, almost a Melville composition in some of the interrogation scenes. Couple that to the involvement of Pierre Étaix and you have a 1970's stretch by Lewis. What if Roberto Benigni had refused to have *Life is Beautiful* released or Robin Williams *Patch Adams*? The world would be a better place, but besides that, the mystery of those two films would not have sewn its roots into our subconscious the way the *The Day The Clown Died* has.

We never know how the death of an artist will hit us. Sometimes an "all is forgiven," or, "why did I take you for granted," other times a gut punch or that hollowing out that comes with the death of a friend. We watch closely that initial year of that loss and are prone to pick up the previously unreleased work, see the final film, read the last book. Years resign themselves to sleeping on top of one another, forgetting where they ended and the one on top of them starts. Another record of previously unreleased tunes, another unauthorized bio, documentaries, repackaging for as long as there is an ember of interest that can sop up the ashes; Bergman at 101 in a Bergman 101 class. In death, the artist truly loses control and in an afterworld glow, we sometimes feel, not think, that we are growing closer to the full picture. Like the thoughts no one else was to know when you were on the phone and some foreign communicative breakthrough allowed that transcript to be translated from the ether; there is so much garbage to swim through to reach your different isles of golden views. It is a nice thought, but a misplaced feeling to think we truly know the intentions and the impetus for any thought, much less strings of them on film. What a wonderful thing to do, as a farewell, promise that your greatest failing could then be unveiled, only the failure shines where it shouldn't and the gawkers are bored out of their minds. I'm dead, but so are you. Ha ha ha.

THE JESUS AND MARY CHAIN
LATE OZU

AN IMAGE, SILENT, and as devastating as the style and color and sound that would come later to you in broken hearts and rage; your last six and first six, in colour, with flashes of red and ankle shots, simple language, an obsession with good mourning TV. Each song and scene seemingly about familial tension, cloaked only by the unique world of its creators who hadn't bothered to clothe the poor things in much of anything other than screams and squeals. The ability to create a singular world, even one that I dislike or do not want to visit like those of Frank Zappa, Todd Solondz, Kate Bush & Henry Jaglom stand taller than others that are simply run-of-the-mill bores. Hear a minute of Coltrane, knowing it is Coltrane right off the bat. Seeing a scene of Godard's, naming that blue hue in a minute. The canon of our favorite artists usually rests on a few concepts that continue to be kicked at, sole scrubbed with dust flying as they try to see better the headstone script, the underneath. That life time of work might only be two notes, like the case of The Jesus & Mary Chain, but what a choice, that pair sewed into the equation then just as the post punk rush of the early to mid-'80s started to map a way to the edge of the midstream; sure, The Mary Chain would be bankrupted by Lollapalooza tours, records that have been called adventureless before imploding after those six records and before the obligatory reunion. But the first couple of pills did what they were supposed to do.

Yasujirō Ozu. Forever reaching, remaking earlier, compact

silent knee plays into elegant full color epics. He was playing a grand—every note, over time, can be heard in his films. His obsessions are on display and recur throughout his filmography, but he also found new tricks and new loves to get infatuated with over the course of his life. It was only in the last five years of his life that the viewer started to track his love affair with the color red. I printed out 30 still shots from these last six films of scenes that were so beautifully and lovingly rended to by his eye, that these once living tableaus now stand as a fine art file in one of my filing cabinets. I lay them out on the wood floor of my house every five years or so to look at them. Seaside red mailbox. Red chair at table with mother and child. Red lamp next to cardboard boxed television. Red shirt on laundry line. Woman towering over two men, red handbag in hand. Red hallway of entry way to bar. Child eating rice out of a red bowl. Red flowers growing out of floating weeds in standing water. Edward Hopper black velvets them back into cartoons. The Jesus and Mary Chain further drive them into pop art. High and Low, early or late era, art is art my caged parrot says as it paints up the newspaper in fresh whites and grays. Touché, I say, hoisting a glass of cabernet in the air, let's agree to agree.

SUICIDE

LIVE 2018

HORROR STORIES, THE EVERYDAY KIND, are the ones that get under my skin. You and yours enter a club in New York City, and it isn't some stupid with a flare gun, but a singer with a motorcycle chain, whipping at the boards. This is the kind of turn-and-run confrontation of the movies, not James Whale's *Old Dark House* so much as the fright of Elia Kazan's *Baby Doll*. Over the top drama that is nearly comedic in its push into a carnival mirror distortion of reality, but the cels aren't animated but the heightened situation is real. Any one of the seven songs on the band's debut record could be used to stunning effect in a horror film; even the beauty of "Cheree" is rendered through a creepy lens thanks to the reverb-drenched vocal that recalls Gene Vincent and the latent/hostile sexuality of the Tennessee Williams screen version of the 1950s. The gothic south replaced by Gotham City. That is Suicide vocalist Alan Vega haunting Andrew Eldritch's post-Wayne Hussey version of that first Sisters of Mercy record, whose name was shortened to The Sisterhood for that one-off 12″, but what the hell is he doing recording a record with Alex Chilton and Ben Vaughn, when he should be credited for his collaborations with Lydia Lunch, Ric Ocasek, Genesis P-Orridge and the nineties electronic band Pan Sonic? Vega was the type of artist that could carve out a world successfully with some of the most difficult collaborators of his generation, oftentimes to stunning effect and at worst leaving the listener with some truly bizarre moments captured on tape that would be hard to fathom had we not the BASF proof. It makes perfect sense that with his collaborator in Suicide, Martin Rev, the two had such a large influence on that bright light marquee Jersey Devil. How many songs in Springsteen's canon are based on films, films that were originally novels, but films are what lay at the root of so many of his songs. "Thunder Road," "Badlands," "The Ghost of Tom Joad" (*Grapes Of Wrath*), "Straight Time," "Atlantic City" (influenced by the Louis Malle film of the same name, strictly conjecture on my part, but some of *King Of Marvin Gardens* seeps into the narrative), "Cautious Man" (*Night Of The Hunter*), "Adam Raised A Cain" (*East of Eden*) and bend this to include some of his better songs that were written specifically for the cinema in "The Wrestler," "Streets Of Philadelphia" and "Limbo." Sometimes people end up where they are supposed to be; Springsteen on Broadway with his definition of terms, Suicide on endless mix tapes and top ten lists.

Suicide was three dimensional cinema that even at this writing with one of their members a few years dead still writhes through yer stereo if you'll only just turn the volume up, a vocal here pushed way into the red, a hushed lullaby that begs you to reach for the knob on your old receiver to get in, get closer to, their music that shakes even the jawbone of a dead blue tooth. For those that stay away from subtitles or piss-stained clubs that birthed Suicide, there is the cinema of Springsteen, portraying the same characters that haunt the drum machine and whirl of the keyboard on Red Star Records. Buy the record then go to the show. They are two wholly different beasts. Maybe you prefer reading the book, then seeing the film. Some writers can't get away from the cinematic. What is cinema anyway but us alone in the dark, alone in the dark in a dream that we will never be in. Ooh-ooh, ah, WHWHHWHWHHAAAEEE.

LEE RANALDO
URINAL URN

MECCA NORMAL WAS PLAYING at The Alligator Lounge in Santa Monica, August 7th 1994, a couple of days after my birthday. I don't recall if our band played that show with them or not, but we had befriended the band by then, booked a number of shows for them in Pomona and both David and Jean had spent the night at our place in San Dimas. I recall that night in Santa Monica that Jean Smith was a bit to the wind after far too many drinks. In the audience, Thurston Moore and Lee Ranaldo had a booth. After the show, I recall Mecca Normal not getting paid their guarantee and Jean Smith attempting to take the cash register to the street. Lee Ranaldo took some liberties writing about the set on his "Skip Tracer" track on Sonic Youth's *Washing Machine* record that came out the following year. I wish Lee had written in the bit about the cash register in the street, punk rock, youth, drunken bravery. Not all of this song is about that eve, or at least, doesn't ring to me of just that night. But then Ranaldo's lyrics always had enough of an obtuse abstraction to call me back for more. There are a lot of vague snapshots on the particle board coffee table, worn out science fiction spines that can't be made out on the shelves of the ghosts and aliens hiding out in the corner liquor stores, unlit in the background of so many of his songs. Caught one, bore witness to the seed of that song being born. Canadians with fangs, not bowing and curtsying to their neighbors to the south. East coast art damaged dawn readers, with their childhood sleeping bags strewn across the kitchen and the den. Do a double take; trace back your steps to find the key. Skip past the banal and all of that night's ticket taking to find what it was you lost, left behind or unwittingly forgot. Just as his ode to Joni got it right on Earth 2, well so too did he get the eye of the Alligator Lounge in "Skip Tracer." Not what I saw, but that is why we have recall built into our minds. I am not looking for a record at the thrift store made up of all of my messages from two decades ago to compare notes with; I already own hundreds of copies of that record.

THE DEAD C
EASY OO'S DELUSION

THEY WOULD PLAY IN SAN FRANCISCO if they were going to play a show in California, but not in Los Angeles. High, in some New Zealand expanse, unwilling to trade in name for cache. It takes will and fortitude to refuse the easiest of check cashing rebates. All of them comedians, studying their craft, living on french fried fast food, how easy to then be on one of them shit marquees? Crap sitcoms, punch-up script rooms, is that what all of those salad days were for? The rent is due, surely, but so are you. We are not expecting you to Lenny Bruce, hyperventilate your court room drama. We understand and are sympathetic. Hell, nearly anyone you talk to will make excuses for Chris Rock's appearances in all of them shitburb Adam Sandler films. Chris Rock, he built up an account with us, we are going to allow him some withdrawals. John Mellencamp, as hard as he tries to flagpole, I know, the guy can afford a million flagpoles. I wish him no ill will, but he is not our kind. He was good looking. He got a 1980 Edith Massey on one of his record covers, but imagine if he had the wherewithal then to have her be the opening act for him on that Johnny Cougar tour. Was it 1980 when he was on SCTV? I ain't going to look it up; I am going to just draw upon memory. Fishing musician, you knew that The Tubes got the punchline, and perhaps Southside Johnny. But Mellencamp? Too early, you gave up your surname. A song of yours called "Hot Dogs & Hamburgers," God Damn. Kenny Aronoff wasn't around to tell you to scratch that scrap? Dylan, who you would later open for, would say the best thing on the record of yours that you hold in highest regard, *Scarecrow*, was the track of your Grandma singing about a dark stormy night. You have to be mindful of all of the traps. Tread lightly. Someone is always handing you something, asking of you to give them your password, your secret handshake.

The virginal post Y2K landscape of this century had us all walking around with afterbirth splattered on us. The new baby, unlearned and impulsive like most of 'em are. That bridge to the 21st century, they wanted to sell it to us real cheap like; cheap like all of those bridges without deeds, handfuls of beads and one dollar bills we pocketed in trade for land rights and civil freedoms. Against a prop bookcase filled with empty paged spines, another state of the union bips and bleeps on like some scratchy 12" on Warp. I was barely present then, in the middle of a children's book that was so engrossing, that it had to be read in one sitting. I can't recall which it was, "We Are Building Toward Something" or "Don't Come Back, Y'all Hear?," but it wouldn't have mattered either one, they would both leave us alone in the same place.

JACKIE MOORE
S/T

JACKIE MOORE LEFT A VOICEMAIL for me at the record store. She was looking to get paid for past royalties owed to her, she said, by the Rhino Records label. The record store in Claremont had not been related to the record label for over 30 years when she called, but what is a fan of Jackie Moore to do but call her back and tell her she had reached the wrong number. That it was neither a lawyer nor a manager, but Jackie Moore doing the footwork, well, that is my kind of an artist. She was so kind and thankful for the call back, we discussed her hit "Precious, Precious" which she has famously said is not her favorite song (she prefers the A-side, "Willpower," not the flip that a DJ turned into a hit for her). We talked about a few other things without my keeping Moore tied up on the phone, she had serious calls to place after all. Moore had the determination in life to leave home early, surrender her college fund and chase after her dream of being an artist. She wasn't simply a talented singer, but a lyricist and tunesmith who co-wrote a number of songs with her cousin David Crawford. She doesn't strike me as one who would give up her publishing or take no for an answer based on her Topps baseball card stats. She took a break from the scene in the mid '70s but was back with some disco before the decade was up prior to dedicating herself to raising her kids, another in a line of things you have to do for yourself. With the kids grown, you might still find Moore on the revival circuit singing some of her and Crawford's hits and deeper cuts (some incredible previously unreleased recordings and deep album cuts from the early '70s appear on the 2015 Real Gone double CD *The Complete Atlantic*

Recordings). She is probably the one changing the oil on the tour bus and setting up the soundboard prior to the show.

Calvin Johnson of K records once had a long-running debt to me that he wasn't paying on after months and months of phone calls (you have to remember, this was years before the VERBOT that chases down known felons and tickles them until the perpetrators uncle themselves to death). Doing it yourself requires tenacity and teeth that cut through dozens of promises of checks being in the mail. I recall offering him the distribution exclusivity on a marquee release that was never going to come out and getting a check in the mail within a week with his thirsty signature. I tell you this now in the event that you ever end up in the same barrel as Jackie or me. I was hoping Jackie Moore did some kind of hat trick and got what was due to her, but then, why am I worried? Of course she did.

LOREN MAZZACANE
+ GREGORY CORSO
S/T

THERE ARE VERY few poets whose voices are married to their work. Sure, most of this has to do with the lack of technological ability to record audio prior to 1860. (A French man, Édouard-Léon Scott de Martinville, beat Edison to it by nearly two decades, glad to report it after every last stitch and staple that Edison tried to copyright as his own.) Sure Burroughs, Maya Angelou, maybe Dylan Thomas or Robert Frost, you may know their voice, but that doesn't mean it is one belonging to the gods. You can argue the point that not one of them owns a golden throat. Gregory Corso has a timbre that I would choose last in the list of those that I would want to read to me on my death bed; his spoken word Harper's audio book for *The Happy Birthday of Death*, let me just see the text instead, Gregory. I was thinking about this while pacing in a V formation, listening to a record by guitarist Mazzacane with vocals by his wife Suzanne Langille, how incredibly moving it was that she was interpreting his playing with her low registering vocals. The bend and depth are all there and in my mind I attribute her deep interpretation and skilled delivery to his rich guitar playing, and him, playing a reflection of her, as one of the most incredible recordings ever made (*Crucible* is a good one, but *Come Night* is where the two of them met their apex). Is it because of the struggle and release of love, the knowing what kind of bread to toast, how to cook the eggs, which side of the bed to sleep on, when to refrain from the language of their banal day to day that allows them to reach so deep into the listener? I first heard them on the local radio station KSPC in 1991, no prior knowledge of either of them, but the track "Take Me Up" was so sensual and otherworldly that I recall pulling my car over and remaining in the car for another ten or so minutes once parked awaiting a back announce so I could find out who it was that had just delivered this to me.

Mazzacane is an artist in no hurry to take you anywhere with most of his playing. His style is mostly unmistakable—be it his attack on the fretboard or the contemplative arcing of the strings on those quieter sketches of songs. Gregory Corso, whose better poems are so ordinary and lacking of the ornate and floral that they read as everyday, I imagined hearing his poems as played on the guitar by Loren Mazzacane (difficult for me to call him Loren Mazzacane Connors or Loren Connors even with it based upon the unfortunate reasoning that "Mazzacane" means killer of dogs in Italian. Something I read a few decades back, about how dogs were always barking at him and he feared being bitten. I could be wrong, but I like this story so I will propagate it). Could I be the editor? Pick the dozen or so poems for Loren to play? Could we put each poem on a separate rice paper insert in each LP sleeve? In my mind, I can do nearly anything, but then here I am, struggling to turn on the light, to get the weeds by their necks to pull up the bulb.

Could *Hearts of Darkness* have been a better documentary (or book) had it been written by any other author of your choosing rather than Eleanor Coppola? *Birthday Letters* by Ted Hughes be more illuminating if written by Anne Sexton? That richness of text that would not exist if de Beauvoir had no Sartre, F. Scott no Zelda, Didion no Dunne, Mary no Percy, Ginsberg no Orlovsky, etc. If you are a writer, think of all of the things that you misheard that became instant poetry. Some crank on the phone asking for a DVD copy of *Voyage To The Bottom Of The Sea* becomes "Voice at The Bottom of The Sea," "Pills to stave off anxiety" becomes "Pills to starve anxiety," and on and on it goes. Now imagine you are an incredibly talented writer and your lover is the most imaginative musician. The two of you improvise, recording religiously, then finely splicing, cutting the diamond, shooing away the ash so that all you have are embers, recording for decades before releasing even a single note. The two of you, and no one else, deciding the sequencing, the cover art, the matrix for the spine and the a/b sides. Free, free from editors, robocall backs, and unimpressed investors. After you are done with them, will you please send along that recording to me? I will send along what I owe in that self-addressed stamped envelope.

DEREK BAILEY/
SUN RA
MERCURIAL

THE BRITISH GUITARIST DEREK BAILEY first appeared to me on a set of records that he recorded with Anthony Braxton on June 29th and 30th, 1974 in London— Wigmore Hall, if it is like any of the Halls that I have visited in Southern California or Philadelphia or Texas, it is one of them gyms of the mind at some University that is closed to the townies and certainly bum banger and mash consumers need not apply. The duo recorded what I imagine is strict improvisation as both records label each side "Set 1" and "Set 2." Braxton on the clarinet and sax with no mathematical equations on the sleeve allowing the listener to connect the dots as to how he came to the entirely fucked conclusions that he does on these two records, as was his wont to do on solo records. The uninitiated listener, or Buddy Rich, or your Grand Funk karaokeing neighbors might hear these recordings and think it is two musicians searching in the dark. They would be right. Searching, and finding some sublime moments, plucked from the ether. No roll of lyrics on the Jumbo-Tron, no set list pushing the three songs that start in D minor away from one another. This is seat-of-the-pants flying.

A few months later, cut-out copies of the 1982 *Yankees* record featuring him, John Zorn, & George Lewis made it to the cut-out bin of my local record store. $4.99? Sure. Put it in the stack with my thirty-seven cent Cheap Tick record & The Last 7". Does this guy have any solo records of just him playing? Yes, of course he does, but often even those are collaborations, like *Music and*

Dance which features his playing matching the movements of dancer Min Tanaka. The 1980 recording features a cover shot of what I imagine is Bailey and Tanaka captured in "human-like settings" the placard next to the concrete jail on Jupiter would read in a foreign language not yet translatable by humans. Listen to the hiss and movement of air eat up a few minutes of time in between some of Bailey's notes. Know that he was capable of playing every bit as lovely as the most musical moments of The Romero Brothers, John Williams, Robbie Basho, or Leo Kottke.

On *Guitar, Drums 'n' Bass*, Bailey does the same thing he was doing with Cyro Baptista, Evan Parker, Cecil Taylor, Tony Oxley and other heroes of mine. He is listening while he is playing; actively reacting without shutting down those ears to make sure his voice is heard. DJ Ninj—some Brit I was not familiar with until this record and have not been familiar with any work of since—is the drum programmer for this record; Breakbeat free jazz from 1995 produced by Bill Laswell. An almost too perfect joke on paper, but holy shit, this record still rips and is like no other that you have heard before.

It was Buckethead, when I asked him what playing with Derek Bailey was like, who replied, "He has huge ears." He meant it both figuratively and abstractly. Bailey was blessed with a pair of ears that were in fact oversized for his sunglassed cranium, and if there is a better listener that painted on the canvas of other musicians as he moved, throw me a note to my PO Box as I would love to hear it.

Sun Ra, yeah, he had some records too.

BLACK RANDY &
THE METROSQUAD
BLACK STAR

GEZA X CAME over to my mom's house when she was away with my stepdad, grocery shopping or some such thing one Friday night. He was with our friend Oskar Meyer whom my brother Allen had met at Chaffey College that first year of his attendance. We knew nothing about Geza at the time; he was a friend of our friend, the way you hope to meet most interesting folks. Allen was eighteen, I fourteen, Geza playing "Hungarian" on my out-of-tune acoustic guitar. He was just another freak from the spiral notebook of my brother's new Chaffey College social life. There was Wally, who later became the artist "Buzzsaw." Wally never broke from his odd Britain-by-Inland Empire accent in his two-tone get up and Wellsian dramatics. There was The Purple Monkey and a host of other pals of his who ended up on one of our cassette-only releases or other. If they didn't already have a nom de plume when they arrived at our doorstep, they got one during any odd recording session. Hell, one tape of ours was a concept record about Allen's friend Ed with the title *Uncle Eddie's Dream Show*, a weird amalgamation of Uncle Floyd and Uncle Sam given to poor Ed whose only taped appearances were a few odd speak-overs and some tambourine playing through a distorted mic into a Peavey amp. Why didn't we record with Geza X? It was customary for nearly anyone that was at our house at that time to end up getting pulled into some improvisational dreck on our Pic 'N' Save cassettes. Well, Geza had that earned air of confidence about him as he played "Hungarian" and a few other songs on my beat up acoustic guitar. Oskar knew other folks in the suburban

IE and LA punk scene at that time, Dinah from 45 Grave, Black Randy, blah blah blah and was quite a raconteur. Most of the folks he knew or had introduced us to had changed their names, so there was no room for us to collar any one of them. He was at our house once or twice a week then, only wanting to hear our Portuguese pressing of *Leave Home*, an old VU record, or *Pass The Dust, I Think I'm Bowie* by Black Randy & The Metrosquad. Allen had picked up his beat up copy of the record that the local La Verne radio station KULV had sold off at Rhino in Claremont five years before I started working there (it had the station's initials as well as programming notes written on the jacket). I don't know if Allen bought it because of the Bowie reference, or having seen the performance of "I Slept In An Arcade" in *Ladies and Gentleman, The Fabulous Stains*. But he bought it nonetheless and it became part of our teenage vernacular. Randy had the exact same shape as all of the weirdos that Allen was bringing into our house at the time, a dash of cartoon pudge on their body & in their language that both hid and revealed the vulnerability and creative instincts just under that. Black Randy still feels to me a part of 1985, not 1979, just as I am sure Bauhaus may feel to younger folks after the fact, like 1997 or 2003. One of the last times I saw Oskar was just after my high school graduation and he mentioned that Randy had AIDS and was not doing well physically or financially. He asked Allen if he could give that copy of the record that we spun to death to Randy as he was going to see him that week. Of course the record was surrendered. The copy that had been thrown to the dustbin by KULV landed in the hands of its rightful owner. How many folks had heard that very copy of that record? How many DJs played it at KULV? How many more heard it? How many lives were slightly set askew by one piece of vinyl that landed at the right place at the right time? I am not even sure of this much, that the record ended back in Randy's hands in time, before he shook off this world and fucked up that great gig in the sky.

ERIC B & RAKIM
S/T

BRING BACK THE HIP HOP DUOS. I love it now, when I hear MF Doom & Slug, Kendrick with Danny Brown, Madlib with Freddie Gibbs, I hunger for entire records; hell, the Kanye & Jay-Z LP is stronger on the West side, but I return to it all the time still. Eric B. and Rakim, those records stand tall still, it is a blueprint worth revisiting and twisting anew. A brand new record of nothing but tracks featuring Kool Moe Dee & Pusha T, pair Syd Tha Kyd with Terminator X at the production helm. There are still a plethora of the architects of hip hop with heels planted on earth that might have a resurgence à la A Tribe Called Quest, who went to bed with one hell of a goodbye kiss. Keep Rick Rubin out of it and let him at Johnny Mathis or Engelbert Humperdinck—Humperdinck as a human piano, stripped-down and doing all the majors and diminished, the black & white keys.

The duo's fourth and final record *Don't Sweat The Technique* was issued in 1992. Large Professor produced the record with the help of Eric B. Mark Harder—whose other work included records by Jimmy Buffett, Max-Q, Koko Taylor and live records by Frehley's Comet and The Descendents—both recorded and mixed the record with Lee Anthony (who at least had his toe in the stream of rap with Brand Nubian, Big Daddy Kane & Souls of Mischief. He was also in the mix by records as varied as those by Tesla, David Bowie, Tiffany, and Giorgio Moroder). Jimmy Buffett and Max Q, well I can't fault the fans for being suspect of at least a piece of this record which in fact turns out to be one of the lesser picks by fans of Eric B. & Rakim, who I will cede were possibly a bit behind the times with a whiff of desperation sniffed out by some in their oxygen tanks. The record has aged gracefully in a dated way, stripped down with lyrics that bounce in the present as prescient then, still holding their water now, and the corners that are dated (including the record cover) still manage to charm as I slide the record out of the preferred poly inner sleeve of the time. How many of them sleeves landed with a crunch, bunched up and unprotective of the vinyl jammed into the spine of the sleeve? Lots, but not mine. Don't sweat the technique.

PRIMITIVE CALCULATORS
KNEE HIGH BLOOD SIGN

PINE CONES AND SCATTERED LIMBS in the high desert, old newspapers, twelve-pack cardboard encasings, rumble trash in the city. Middle of nowhere fires. These had been our hallmark. From the collected campus of no school, you might see thousands of us in your lifetime and not know that we are a union. Like the century beetle that is birthed for just a small window every eighty to ninety years, you don't know it is there until your peripheral vision registers something on the far left. On the lip of nothing, circled, facing one another, we are exhausted. None of us say a thing. On our aluminum chair webbing watching the flame dance, irises contracting as the flame grows. The fucking things whizzing by our heads, hitting our foreheads, arms, stuck in our hair. Attracted by smoke and heat and light, swarming our site, landing on the embers, roasting their hulls, black marshmallows puffing out like cornered cats as they enfold the fire, so many of them that it didn't take much for us to put the damn thing out before a quick retreat into our tents. I had never heard of such a thing. But then, what little I had taken in in entomology didn't lend itself to real world insects. Not the kind that we would encounter deep into the dark and certainly not these foreigners immolating their shells.

We are little bands. Small enough to move nimbly, without notice, so entirely asterisked that were we to do such a thing, it is doubtful that it would even be noticed. Bored kids with bottom rung tools; red plastic microphones with on/off switches plugged into 40 watt amps; "Can you hear me now?" said over and over again before cellular trap doors destroyed the meaning of that phrase. "Turn the bass down....TURN THE BASS DOWN." The outback is just like your backwoods or your wrong side of the tracks. Every city has one, even if it is just one lone house with residents that don't belong with their brethren, or who are ostracized, clowned down. Those that can't get an art school escape sometimes create them fascinating milk retardant pieces of work that cannot be taught, cannot be learned. These things have to grow under just the right light for the right amount of time, and because of the extended time it takes to make such things, the risk is too great to purposely put your child through seventeen or eighteen years of that. Gestating. Crushed chrysalis, monarchs flapping around for nine months before they themselves become the wind. We know their cycles, these RPMs that are signaling from the middle of nowhere, they sound like us and our friends, but these things are difficult to parse from the UR90 transmissions that we can reach only in the late eves nightly. I am trying to stay up; I am Donald Sutherland horror movie concerned, I mean both of them.

BLACK SABBATH
DEAD AGAIN

BLACK SABBATH'S *BORN AGAIN* was released in 1983. The cover art by Steve Joule was submitted as a joke, a plea to not use it because it was so ridiculous, and simultaneously a drunken bust up with a neighbor of his. The artwork stands in my mind as one of the finest Charleston comic pop art record covers ever created. Throw a $.12 tag with an "approved by the comics code" flag beneath it, crumple up the top right edge, and you really have something. I would pay admittance to that comic book brought to the big screen as a fourteen-year-old. I would buy that record, just as I bought Nazareth's *No Mean City* or maybe a Molly Hatchet record, just for the cover. I did buy that record, hell, I bought all three. That Nazareth record sucked then, and it sucks now. I remember my father having what I imagined then were powers of ESP when he questioned me about buying that Nazareth record. "You're buying it for the cover artwork, aren't you?" The cover art by Rodney Matthews— famous for his Asia and Rick Wakeman cover art since—was in fact the only selling point. That image was the entire one sheet, the whole of the sizzle reel, the hit song. I knew nothing about the Scottish band Nazareth, couldn't as a ten-year-old put two and two together that theirs was the hit versions of Boudleaux Bryant's "Love Hurts." God damn it, a week's allowance throw for a crap LP in a magnificent pre-teen boy dream (ditto for Molly Hatchet). But Black Sabbath's *Born Again* is such a nasty sounding and looking record that even all the bloated alcoholic fatty tissue swelling up around the thing, the filthy lagoon of murky production and some god awful lyrics cannot stop this beast from being a fantastic listening (and viewing) experience.

Ian Gillan, who sings on the record, not only purportedly said he vomited when he saw the cover art, but also crashed drummer Bill Ward's car while recording the record (the first cut on side one, "Trashed," is Gillan's retelling of this event in song). What a disastrous turn joining Black Sabbath turned out to be for him. Gillan didn't even realize, over a drunken eve with Tony Iommi, that he had joined Black Sabbath until the morning after hangover call from his manager. Hunh? I did what last night? Yeah, well, what the hell did you or I do last night that could be as funny as that? Other stories abound that this wasn't supposed to be a Black Sabbath record at all, but that at the insistence of the record label, the band name was sewn onto the jacket. Poor Bill Ward, everything you read about the guy is about how he was the butt of far too many jokes during his tenure in Sabbath and then when you cap it off with the new singer totaling his car, well it makes me want to send a bouquet of flowers to him on behalf of all of the shade thrown his way.

"Zero The Hero" may be one of the worst music videos ever made—goats, chickens, *Invasion of The Body Snatchers* Glad-wrapped bodies, Adolf Hitler? The video employs the scariest use of chickens since Willy Wonka and the best use of lobotomized surgeons in a C horror film in a music video circa 1983. Shock ending, the Frankenstein monster is a music critic that drinks catsup, eats eggs and gets a Dracula red badge of courage as the track fades. It is just incredible that this footage ended up being used when the intercut concert footage would have sufficed. Talk about stream of conscious unedited thought. Lyrically and musically, the song could have been on that Royal Trux record that David Briggs produced. Butt rock with noncommercial leanings, muddy pants, everyone kind of too fucked up and hazy to bring any of the chapters to a close. The entire record plays this way. No one was truly invested and there was no one around that—in the flurry of writing, recording, sequencing or turning in the cover art—seemed to have had the energy to say no to any of it. This is as close as I imagine any band comes to being a democracy, of utilizing whatever is at hand. Everyone in the band so exhausted and uncommitted that the "first idea, best idea" idiom is the only rule of the day. Sure, the record is a mess, but there are so many oddly inspired moments or unique things happening over the course of the thing, that I have never put this one to bed. I revisit it religiously. Not my favorite Black Sabbath record, but still my favorite Black Sabbath record. Even during my most litmus-testing of tastes at seventeen, twenty and twenty three, it never got thrown into the discard pile. In 2011 when the expanded two-disc CD was issued, I was there. The disc adds an outtake; an expanded version of the "Stonehenge" instrumental (again, was anyone at the wheel here?) plus a live set featuring pandering live tracks covering Purple & Sabbath standards on the bonus disc ("Iron Man," "Smoke On The Water," "Paranoid" of course) to which Gillan says he could barely memorize the lyrics, and at not so close listen, he is correct. The set includes 4 tracks from the then newly unveiled *Born Again* performed live, which in this day and age is a rarity. Marquee bands may throw two songs from their new record into a set but dare not slow down the proceedings when there are seats to sell and merch to unload. I mention this not to sell you on a two-disc set, but to shine a light on the haphazard delivery of every aspect of this version of the band. So many things here are not right, and for that I am eternally thankful.

GREEN ON RED
MOTEL LIVES

I APOLOGIZE, DEAR READER, for slipping into nostalgia, that disease which has so infected our current culture that it is difficult for us to drive past all of its exits on the highway to get to the new without veering into one of its well-lit tourist trappy nappys. It is a diseased illusion that comforts us when we instead should be searching for new ways to sit and stand and walk, tossing away chairs with four legs for the preferred one legged chair and .05-a-cycles that we ride into town. However, I drew up a make-believe front cover for an imagined Green on Red cassette and as Green on Red are a part of my DNA, even if it was for only one fleeting summer, I cannot write about them without disclosing how they became so entwined with my twisty defective railroad track dead-ending strand that is thankfully unique to me. I am so close to one of their records that it is beyond reproach. Summer of 1985, I was fifteen soon to be sixteen, fresh off of picking up The Replacements' *Let It Be* at Licorice Pizza. I plunked down $6.99 for Green on Red's *Gas Food Lodging* on a return visit to that same store. The clerk at the record store that I had a crush on asked if she could open the record up to see the green vinyl it was pressed on, as she had never seen green vinyl. Before I could respond with a teen soaked Frank Nelson "Y-E-E-E-S-S-S," she added that she would take a dollar off if I would allow her to split the seam. I was five months from losing my virginity, but when she slid her nail down the sleeve and pulled that green vinyl out of the jacket, I think my cherry area turned six shades brighter.

I was years away from Jimmy Rodgers, The Bristol Sessions,

Charley Patton, et al. when I first heard "That's What Dreams," the lead off track on the record. A perfect song. A song that begins the record with stripped down aching solo guitar leads into the shadowland of crushed hopes and dreams with a then newly-into-adulthood Dan Stuart reaching deep on the vocals. My brother and I pored over this album, and that summer, only one year into writing songs together as The Bux, we recorded our first stabs at country songs, such stinkers as "Lady I'm a Bad Man," "Train Train," and other even less notable songs on BASF 120 tapes. Like any decent archeologist, the thread of Green On Red led to poor buying choices of far too many records on the Enigma Label imprint (Jet Black Berries was one and my disappointment with Plasticland whose record was produced by Paul Cutler, also at the helm of *Gas Food Lodging,* was another. Cutler was in the band 45 Grave and latter-era Dream Syndicate, so cut him a break for this minor misstep) but some diamonds as well (Redd Kross, Tex And The Horseheads, Rain Parade, Chris D.).

Green on Red's affectation had a charm to it, that unlike artists whose records I bought while attending Montclair High over the next 2 years and later cringed at (Tom Waits, Elvis Costello, and The Dream Academy) still charms me today. Even the clumsy cover of "We Shall Overcome" is forgiven. I would get them same red on green shivers five years later when I heard the song "Wrecking Yard" by Chris Cacavas that he recorded in between Green On Red records, as perfect a break up song as has ever been penned. Where much of *Gas Food Lodging* succeeds is in even its darkest moments it doesn't make you feel so alone in this world, "Wrecking Yard" delivers the flipping coin answer, responding, ah, that was all just an illusion.

LEONARD COHEN
SONGS FROM OUR ROOM

PART ONE

The best comedians look like him. And my favorite comedians deliver their very personal tragedies and heartaches in a manner that does not give short shrift to the pain of those mended parts of him. There they are, right before you, hanging from the oversized trunk, unpruned, growing wildly before everyone in the household with no one thinking to tend to it, to maybe get an arborist over to that stumpy overgrowth (if you live in the suburbs), a hacksaw if you reside on the lower end of that demarcation line. Nah, we just let you grow through the chain link and because of them Santa Ana winds, your left side leans to the right making you appear like you are always curious about how someone parked or what they are trying to communicate to you.

PART TWO

Cohen is one of the artists of whom, if you are a listener, you do in fact bear witness to his inner world; thoughtful, empathetic, oversexed, depressed, spiritual, a searcher. How many friends were on the payroll simply because they needed financial support? I know of at least two, and certainly there were more. In the late '90s when Cohen made his home for much of that time at the Zen Center in Mt. Baldy, just up the street from where I worked, he would be around town. You would see him eating at the Greek restaurant, at the local bakery and once in a while in the local record store. Everyone from Morrissey, Iggy Pop, Gene Simmons, and Tom Waits has been through the doors of the store, but no one, other than some non-famous customers, had that aura of announcing themselves without the need for attention. There was Cohen checking out the Leonard Cohen section to see if the outside world still noticed while he was far into retreat mode.

PART THREE

I imagine Cohen having had a million ideas for films, unfortunately none of them were fleshed out and they all run from a paltry thirty seconds to a maximum of two minutes long, and to further exacerbate the likelihood of them every being produced, they are fantastical and costly affairs to bring to the silver screen for just 120 seconds which is why he never got funding for them.

THUMBNAIL I

Á twenty-seven-year-old on a rubber raft in Joshua Tree takes an Elk Ridge hunting knife out of her fanny pack and stabs the desert. A stream of fresh water gushes forth. Cut to three years later, her floating on a Robinson Crusoe tree house in the middle of the Indian Ocean which has drained into California. She is deep spear diving. With goggles on and weathered scuba gear skin-tightened, her head thrusts out of the water. Taking the breathing apparatus out from her mouth and screaming out to a river rafter with arms pulling her onto her 18th century float, she cries out "Dang cacti, cut up my flippers."

THUMBNAIL 2

An alien body snatcher begins its plan for world domination by first taking over the hulls of every head pharmacist at even the lowest Podunk drugstore hidden in the jungles of Borneo. In every prescription, a slow time-release dose of merthamedalflum is added. Over the course of six months, everyone on the drug becomes a self-involved artist and announces it by their dress, language, and choice of eye wear. The fucking thing is a 1918 rerun, coming in second and third waves as more and more folks were affected by the contaminated water wells or mutated viruses. Thinking it the time for the great reveal, the aliens unmask via a dispatch from overhead and claim themselves to be God almighty. A worldwide atheist shrug and a "so what" is followed by a worldwide "Let's move on to our oobydoobest era" in all fields of the arts. Aliens? Gods? Check out this macrame'd table cloth that will cut at you while you eat off of it one artist says to the other whose response is, oh no, I'm only an aura, I can't feel anything.

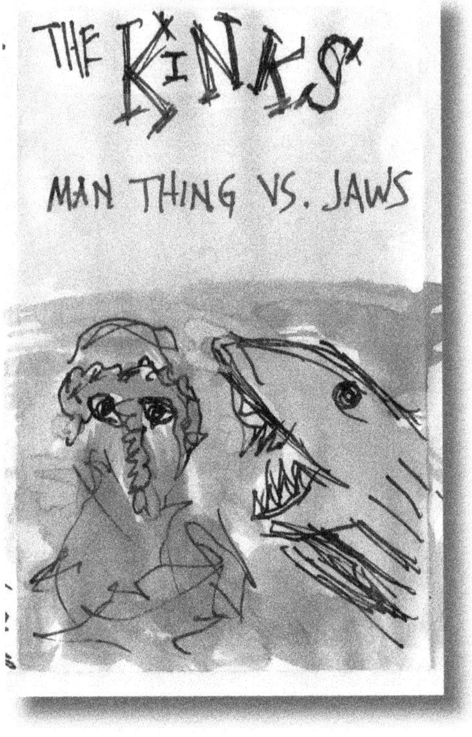
THE KINKS
MAN THING VS. JAWS

THE KINKS
THAT DAMN MAN
THING VS. JAWS

MARVEL COMICS VS. DC COMICS. The Submariner to the shadow of Aquaman; the X-Men towering over The Teen Titans; Swamp Thing's deeper lasting roots than that of Man-Thing; Deathstroke into Deadpool. Nova's mid-seventies design painted over The Green Lantern. Rocket Racer's skateboard to The Silver Surfer's wall hanger of a longboard. Maybe if you were a comic book reader, you hold these creations in high regard, so please take this with a grain of salt. If you can find it in you to forgive me for liking Jack Kirby's Devil Dinosaur, well, you win this high stakes game of nonjudgment where the stakes are so very low. Had Devil Dinosaur been a larger hit, he would be a few sentences north of here played against DC comics Kamandi, another Kirby creation whose origin and story arc bares more than a similar resemblance to that of Devil Dinosaur. Where there is success, there are knock-offs. Poor dead Bruce, the mechanical shark in *Jaws*, his spawn would include *Mako*, *Tintorera*, *Great White* and other species with the same behavior problems (*Tentacles*, *Orca*, *Alligator,* and up out of the water onto terra firma, there was *Grizzly*, *Dogs* and even them cute little bunnies turned ferocious for the sake of commerce in *Night Of The Lepus*). The longtime parlor game of pitting those of equal powers against one another at the peak of their game spans arena after arena. There are of course instances where in real time these dream fights did occur. The Kinks were one of them. Two talented songwriters in the same band, fighting to keep the band together as they one upped each other trying to gain control of the pecking order and that of the leader of the band with the music listening audience on the strength of their songs, looks, performance, demeanor... whatever trick it would take to win the damn thing. *Lola Versus Powerman and the Moneygoround* released in 1970 was a record filled with odd superheroes and villains. "Lola," the reticent hero of the future, "Apeman," another misanthropic entry in the Davies songbook and "Powerman," like many of the songs on the record, references the band's legal and financial troubles at the time, could have just as easily been penned by Jack Kirby about Stan Lee.

Ray Davies, and Dave as well, were writing records filled with nostalgia and themes of commerce railroading art while other bands were wearing beads and trying on their first bells. For all of the histrionics of their sibling rivalry on and off stage, the two of them had plenty in common insofar as their experience in the music biz, what they were up against and what they were just plain against. The Everlys, The Bee Gees, The Beach Boys, CCR, The Jesus and Mary Chain, those dudes in The Black Crowes, the Gallaghers, sure, they all had feuding brothers like The Kinks. The Kinks, however, are the first entry in this category for how wide and how long the rivalry lasted. The deeper you dig, it is more than just onstage fisticuff break ups, song positioning on LPs, photo shoots, marred wedding days and 50th birthday celebrations gone awry by the Davies brothers, but these outbreaks were not relegated to the two of them against one another. Drummer Mick Avory has been in physical and mental scuff-ups with each of the brothers, and you don't have to dig deep into the lyrical make up of The Kinks canon to see and hear dozens and dozens of battles taking place. I would posit that the entire foundation of The Kinks is built upon what they are not as opposed to defining who they were. Ray's "I'm Not Like Everybody Else," the B-side of their "Sunny Afternoon" single from 1965, was as much a mission statement as the hit single's much-loved flip. The band's trajectory from '67 to '71 then past that golden hour, them odd records released through to 1977. The span is as stunning as The

Beatles jump over nine years. *Something Else, Village Green, Arthur* followed by the aforementioned *Lola Versus, Muswell Hillbillies,* the weirdo theater of *Preservation Act 1 & 2,* the half-baked *Soap Opera* and the better *Schoolboys In Disgrace* up to 1977's *Misfits* which generally defined their mood and direction for the next decade. What these records lack in delivery, they make up for in ambition compared to what them Liverpudlian ne'er-do-wells accomplished. Sure, the early Kinks records are beyond reproach at this late a date, as beyond as anything can be anyway, but this wingspan lays bare their idiosyncratic and perverse use of language, concepts and musical choices before they got on course for their commercial act Part 2 from the late '70s to the mid '80s. The commercial potential of pop art was on the precipice of smashing glass ceilings with larger million-selling platters, blockbuster films; comic books still just a glint in the eye of the latter. There was a softness around the edges of freshly broken ground where the blood of commerce was being sniffed out of orifices, mined and its waste thrown against the wall Kubrick monkey style. The Kinks bemoaned all of this over multiple tracks on records leading up to, and even following, the ushered-in bean counter procession as the seventies gave way to the eighties which were ripe then for corporate kill jars. Collect them all, the foil covers, the direct editions, the hardcover reissues, it doesn't matter; they are all monster stories, and no one truly ever lives or dies in them make-believe pages. Check out any bio of any artist, feel the seam of their scars, the fractures and the psychotic breaks with reality. This Man-Thing is a total drag.

RONNIE DOVE
WHAT THE FUCK IS WRONG WITH ME TODAY

TIP OF THE HAT to any artist that is still writing or playing music after the age of sixty. Double that if you are Ronnie Dove who posted this missive on Facebook on December 5, 2017:

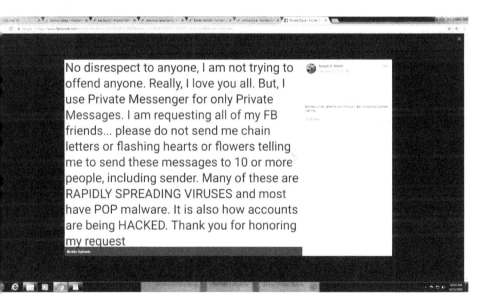

> No disrespect to anyone, I am not trying to offend anyone. Really, I love you all. But, I use Private Messenger for only Private Messages. I am requesting all of my FB friends... please do not send me chain letters or flashing hearts or flowers telling me to send these messages to 10 or more people, including sender. Many of these are RAPIDLY SPREADING VIRUSES and most have POP malware. It is also how accounts are being HACKED. Thank you for honoring my request

KANYE WEST
COLLEGE DEBT

YOU GAVE THEM FIRE, fire for their bon mots. Clever in *The New Yorker*, brief and broken online. Take the ammunition of their personal life and apply it to their water-colored stillborns, water coolered Monday sulks. Everyone is a critic. Your work is not enough. We must also delve into your private life. It is not enough, the bits that you surrender. Those crumbs even from an acquaintance would be worth ten times the dime that we value it. To cheapen and draw false equivalencies, it is easier than to create anew something of our own making. Charles Bronson, his mom dressed him as a girl. He, for his Jewish heritage, was mocked ceaselessly. Yet there he is, appearing. Right there in Sergio Leone's *Once Upon a Time In The West*, harmonica in his mouth, hanging. John Huston, Jill Ireland, & Randy Quaid surrounding him in 1975's *Breakout*. What must he have then thought? With his trailer and his craft services catering? They going to yell out "Jew boy"? "Nancy man"? Go on ahead. Hard scrabbled, we are, with new names. We owe no one nothing. We read none of your fanzines pissing themselves into an ezine frenzy. Listen to none of your body snatcher broadcasts that became podcasts. We are in the desert deserting this world as quickly as we can.

I don't expect you to delve into the body politic or follow sports. I don't look to you to give me dating advice nor stock tips. I don't know your children's names, the lineage of your wife's family, I don't have time to follow or like or push or point. The silencing of voices and opinions, even uninformed opinions, are these what we are making all of these pillow cases for online? Muffled and sewn over images and thoughts that aren't similar to our own?

Bryan Ferry hunting foxes, I still listen to Roxy Music, all the miscreants and abusive sway of the punk rock scenes and the swinging London beads and the hillbilly white lightning. All of them anti-heroes, thugging and thieving if only in the believe-make, are they a reflection of you and I? There are mean-spirited artists everywhere. Todd Solondz, Yorgos Lanthimos... I've seen their films which hit me like Irwin Allen spectacle as one dimensional and histrionic without any depth of substance. So what? I think twice before seeing another of their films, but I won't be writing letters nor doing anything short of this about them and what I find as their artistic shortcomings. They are struggling to get their voices heard. I applaud even the most foul of souls that creates art of any kind. It is our duty to fly up the flagpole the gold, ignore the dreck, and sure, shine a light on what gets to our solar plexus. Kanye? I couldn't care less about everything about him save for his records. I don't know him, I won't meet him, I don't need some personal connection with him that I have beyond what is there when it is just his record on and me listening. Do I have to argue that point again? Yeah, yeah I do, I live in a college town. I practically have to explain why I ain't slowing down for that idiot silver spooning his way outside of a crosswalk. If I hit him, it's his fault. My mom taught me that.

West's towers are not shell games or babel monologue to nowhere, husks of gold with nothing inside of them. I slide any number of his records out of the sleeve and they speak to me. He has arguably released two of the greatest hip hop records in the history of the genre. OK maybe three. Hold on, possibly four.

MEATLOAF
ASSHOLE IN THE SENATE

NORMAN MAILER, ATTEMPTING to push his imagined girth through the sheets of femininity. Tough guys don't dance, and fucking is dancing, see. Is that what trips you up? All that soundproof carpeting? You then a middle-aged Frankenstein monster plucking daisies, a scribe for Penguin writing a book on Marilyn. The only part of it you understood was the pillside strangle, the gurgle. No one asked for you bedside. Arguing with lepers about how Lazarus truly felt as he came back to. You, dust covered, relegated to a previous century now that you are done poking fun at Capote and Jong, you needed to be read so fug was nickeled in where fuck should have been. You man of men, circle jerking your V-10 engine, confusing more with less, adding further curbside asphalt to the ring of the fire thinking that it will help to warm you. We'd been around your kind all of our lives. It wasn't courage or grit that burnished us, smoothed out our piranha bite. It was that simple equation of asshole versus underdog. You, you got none of our noise, so you get none of our noise. To you, we expressed then not a note of your world. We knew you. We had read you. In your decline, I am sure that some of us even laughed at you. Not me, I am not yet that unkind. "Second rate Jack London." "Boxing rink Dixie cup." "Jockstrap undercarriage from the Earl Scheib paint job modeling agency." "Slow motion loan revealed."

A blackened list gold medalist hooping every net and every jump, we could see then, even with our low definition wattage. The well-paid pole vaulters, chain link charging the surroundings at your lift-off. The feigned solitude masked curtains surrounding your uterine A-List. Into the theater you go, with your burger cheese fries and pockets of candy. You can watch, but you will never see how the film was made. Pugnacious, like all of them Men's men, we were 16 or 18 and thought then when we read your books that we just hadn't read enough yet to understand you. There, in the shadows of night, there are softer corners that you did go, and even in your book on Monroe, when you aren't dancing around DiMaggio and Arthur Miller, there is a soft side there. There, when you talk about Bobby Kennedy. We can read interviews and we can read novels, but you have to learn to read faces and body language and small font asides to see the vulnerabilities that may be so worked on that they are fighting your every visit to appear not to exist.

THE EX &
TOM CORA
BIG GAME HUNTER DONNY JR.

EVERYONE HAS THEIR OWN RELIGION, even those of us that would be hard-pressed to relate to you what exactly our religion is. If you don't belong to one of the three hundred or so varying houses or sects, there is still a home for you, one maybe stronger, or sicker than those other choices, but we all reside within a set of beliefs. Anton LaVey rewrote the bible and it reads like an even worse book than the ones written by Ayn Rand. You can define yourself with the terms of your defined aggressors, or even the flip of those terms. What kind of antidote do we then have if we are to refrain from being stuck-in-the-mud reactionaries? By the time I was fifteen, punk rock was doing 1984 time. It was in fact 1984, and there were dress codes and bros, straight edges and Exploited, *Maximum Rock 'n' Roll* rants by fashion rats accusing one another of bubonic leanings. You can never be too rigid; you can never be too far in. I skipped out on the course on Crass, and second generated to The Ex, Dog Faced Hermans, and the other Dutch post punk agit rhythms that were born out of that egg. The Ex had been birthed in The Netherlands in 1979. *Aural Guerrilla* was released in 1988, and was the gateway drug entry for me. Intriguing in its angularity and mission, minus a bit of the litmus condescension, it rested there in a wood crate and greeted me warmly when in 1991 I placed next to it their record with cellist Tom Cora, *Scrabbling At The Lock*. What a perfect amalgamation of world music, outsider jazz, AMM noise as language and punk rock. I didn't belong to no temple, had no rigid core that would forbid my veering this way or that, and at the time, the inclusive rage of The Ex had its doors open, and it didn't smell like warmed over venison or overwrought doctrines. Middle aged, and ire rises still. I create new songs by The Ex in my head at least once a month. One is about the 1%. another is about that asshole in his Prius driving twenty in a forty, something us lefties and righties can agree on. The last one is always a song of praise from the hymnal of a village idiot.

CARL REINER & MEL BROOKS
THE 2045 YEAR OLD MAN
CHRIS KNOX
NO

C HRIS KNOX WOULD have really been something had
he been born earlier so as to appear on *Your Show of Shows*
or *The Dick Van Dyke Show* or had Mel Brooks turned over rocks
and given the young New Zealander the roll of Dr. Frankenstein
that was secured by Gene Wilder in *Young Frankenstein*. Check
the song by his and Alec Bathgate's pre Tall Dwarfs band Toy
Love entitled "Bride of Frankenstein" where, quite possibly due
to this oversight, the video features Knox in the role of the good
doctor. Knox's songwriting prowess is matched by his wicked sense
of humor that is best on display in his live shows. Knox would
not only deliver knock 'em dead hilarious lines that the audience
would be hard-pressed to believe were improvised on stage, but
burst quasar into the audience and interact/subjugate 20-some-
things standing there with arms folded. It was not uncommon
for folks to step back à la Gallagher when Knox got to the lip of
any given stage and started to make his way through the club.
One of the few dozen shows of his that I saw had Knox mashing
a found banana on himself then audience members, a hilarious
play on Iggy and peanut butter or Darby and his razor blades. He
was Robin Williams without the coke manic corybantic sweat and
need for adoration; no two shows were the same. My brother and

I took a walk with Chris onto Sunset Boulevard before a show on November 1, 1993. I believe Chris Jones, the drummer among many other things in Refrigerator, was there as a third witness as we came to the door of The Viper Room where there was a fresh makeshift shrine for River Phoenix who had passed away the day before. Among a small gaggle of bereaved teenage girls and tourists, Chris went into a bit on Hollywood, death, flowers and cellophane that would make any comedian jealous with its stark punch punctuated by a jaw-dropping audience of we three and the tourists who were teary-eyed in sorrow for River. No laugh out loud guffaws for Knox from this audience, and three folks there were biting down on lower lips out of respect to the mourners. Holy shit, this is no act, and this guy is for real. Maybe that is why he took offense at what no one else in the world has ever taken offense to, Ira Kaplan's weirdly beautiful worm dance that is on display at times when Kaplan plays the keyboard live for Yo La Tengo. Knox said "It wasn't dangerous enough; he needs to disarm the crowd." I told Chris that I didn't think the point of what Ira was doing in performing live music was danger, and Knox replied that "Of course it is, live music is dangerous." I have seen some incredible live shows that absolutely had no hint of danger in them and they didn't leave me wanting for it. It was humor that I saw weaving itself in to both of their sets. Yo La Tengo with less bludgeon and bombast than Knox, but it is there, amply. Comedy and music are two places where real time love and hate collide in performance. Chris Knox and the trio of Yo La Tengo are right up there in my ledger of some of the best comedians of their generation, I mean, better than Rita Rudner, Gallagher and Kip Addotta, for real. Their courage, love and commitment were and are beyond reproach.

The through line of comedy through music is so omnipresent that it is invisible. Even in the doldrums-scripted world of arenas and award shows, you will find comedy used as a method to connect with an audience or to defuse tension after a ballad or intense song. This is a comedy all its own, like some shitcom or weak Chevy Chase *Funny Farm* kind of "comedy" that those with a toe into the depth of the thing would be hard-pressed to find a laugh in. You will find *Funny Farm* filed in the "comedy" section, but it isn't comedy at all. Just like Ulysses S. Grant was "presidential" or Wal-Mart is a "gathering place." These are lazy places to lay things that no one really cares about, like them bikes and scooters that litter the sidewalk of downtown. No one wants them, and they don't know where to get rid of them or hide them.

Not a word has been written about a great comic without the first word being "timing." The same counting down of the present into the past is invaluable in music. Timing is what sets apart so many artists that have an idiosyncratic sense that belongs to them alone, that a few seconds into their music, you can call it as them. The Shaggs, Moondog, Thelonious Monk, Half Japanese, early Germs, Al Green's before or after the beat delivery, Elvin Jones behind Coltrane, all of them have a time signature that does not follow 4/4 or fusion/prog mind-bending 3/7 into 6/9. These things that we do for each other at parties to make one another laugh, well, sometimes they are just done to fill up space between the hands. Other times, they are truly funny. Reiner and Brooks, cracking up their peers with off the cuff riffs on a two thousand-year-old man. Their love of Ravel and Schubert and Count Basie. Reiner as Chopin, Mel Brooks singing "High Anxiety" or directing Gene Wilder's idea of having Frankenstein sing "Putting On The Ritz" or any number of musical moments that dot his films. He was, after all, a drummer. Imagine what Mel Brooks looks like behind a trap. Throw Sid Caesar up in front of him on the sax (which Sid was competent at) and then get Carl Reiner to sing his Pagliacci. Free jazz classical music is born. Step aside Charlie Ives and Igor Stravinsky, this bird is on fire from the inside out and is about to explode. Run, run up the boroughs, flipping the finger and laughing down your skidded knees while screaming "So long, 174th Street, I can't afford you anymore, thank God!"

THE MOVE
TINA'S GROWING PILLOW

WASHED OUT TECHNICOLOR REPEATS, they start to lose their feeling if you aren't careful. Nothing but oranges, reds, auburns. They can't fade to black, that cartridge is all used up. It just breathes a heavy sigh on the line, one misread as sexual when it is truly just resignation. The stronger colors, they are smart enough to decline. To retreat. To stop showing themselves to even you, you well-cordoned off houser of secrets. It was an open set, but the trailers in the back were off limits. Here, where we were trading pills. Dioramas, our suitcases, housing souvenired losses that we hauled from Oslo to Helsinki, customs abandon, passports failing like kidneys and hearts do, like future strangers do. You can recall me from way back then if that is easier for you to do than to look at me, look at me now. But I am here, now. Right before you. There is no admittance beyond this point. Not for you. Not for your party. Costumes, stage clothes, well-practiced banter megaphones announcing your every arrival. A skunk in the highway divide whose entrails open to exhale. Don't let them in. Don't let me in. I quit. Find me park benched. Dog-eared on a coiled telephone. A lottery winner of regret. There are well-lit exit signs, open your eyes; they lay not only in front of you, but deep down there in the cheap seat hind. Walk past the past. You in your stacked parting cocktail dress. God damn it, I thought that you might have learned at least that one good trick I did, in the time that you spent with me. French exits. Disappearing acts. Some of your entourage went on to be knighted, but you, you ducked that epee blade, you with your cunning MBE rental that you lightning speed returned to the queen. Dear sir or madam, this is not for you to look upon. Back to your crumb fleck mote, provincial local news section life and times. Washed out Technicolor repeats, they are losing even their feelings. There are some of us in this very group who are so low, so low to the ground that we can hear the whispers, the wants, the desires and yearns of our ages. It is with the strength of the heavens that we turn away. Home, home, leave home. Home, home, don't return. Why would we want to go back there, stacks of old TV guides, rooms that not only we, but lodgers as well, dare not live in any longer? We are now thick with pills and sleep, throw pillow hand-me-downs. Comforted by the tea and vee. It is not right or natural for us to age gracefully after living such sordid lives. Kick the cane out from beneath, the roar from your still almost-all-there vocal folding organs. We don't care. We didn't come here to live out our last few days peacefully, our arms, right now, this very second, are thrown akimbo welcoming extinction. Extinction, don't not show and make me look the fool.

THE SUN CITY GIRLS

PLEASE JESUS, I JUST NEED AN ESCAPE

SAW YOU OUT WITH YOUR BOYFRIEND today, with his cane and his fangs. Is that a costume or a disease? Something he wears to keep quiet his halo? You never know, any of our exes could have been my best friend had they not landed on that axis so close to we two. A king without a throne is served so easily. Served repeatedly at a restaurant where the waiters serve as servants and the patrons speak easy over the hardcore. Bring along someone to soften up the edges, and another to the table to bleed. We got Xs on our hands, fake IDs, iconography that we are turning on its head so as to not be read. You have to move quickly, be nimble, discard so fast that every symbol and font and style of handwriting before your births become unusable. You only get in once, to this bar. The well wishes of watered-down thinks are made up of planks, some walk off seemingly with no warning, mid-sentence. But then, you are new, and this all to you, is all new too. The queen sits at home, shown on one of them 1989 big screens. Primary colors project her blowing out candles on a home shopping spree. Flame retardant hippies, make-shifting reality with their Owsley, turquoise jewelry, washing themselves in the mud and cum of Woodstock. Bill Graham's vampiring leaches bleeding them into the soft underside of disease, turning them on with fringe suede vests, leather mufflers, blood free uppers.

A decade later, we were left with ash and shit-stained shoes. Horrible underground comics, tired reformative versions of your bands that were spoon fed on the "FM free" band in between ads for water beds, Styrofoam black beauties and old Millhouse masks. Phoenix Arizona, 1979, the brothers Bishop and pals form The Sun City Girls. Year zero. If you have heard nary a note of their music, you can actually piece it together by the names of the record labels they were on: Placebo, Majora, Eclipse, Amarillo and finally their own Abduction label. Their early begin of taking a piss out of the mysticism, I Ching, eastern lean, numerology, UFO sightings, Jim Jones cult parties and late seventies embers of remembrance of late sixties culture, all can be heard in their unique brand of punk rock free jazz improvisational Takoma nods. Shorthand. We only have so much time here together, and it is not my intention to write a report about The Sun City Girls. There are some bumps in the road, some illness and death, but it is generally a happy ending with a ton of smaller roads to venture out on once their highway ends. I don't want to spoil any of it for the previous non-listener or the shoulder hunched care lessers. You'll have to trust me. Follow the sign after the Lance Burton disappearing act for approximately one mile, then take a sharp right.

DOROTHY ASHBY
THE MOVING FINGER (20-MINUTE VERSION)

THEY MAY SAY STAY POSITIVE, do the best you can. Sometimes, though, the best thing to do is to say no. You can always say no. That desert we spent a weekend's allowance on populating that sand with fortune cookie seeds. It takes time. Eventually you will get to the root, maybe even the bloom. We followed a mass transit train in my beat up El Dorado. Me on the 210, it on a third rail; I wanted only to see where it ended. Such a fool, such a fool am I. It ends at every stop. It stops at every light. Is that what I am supposed to be doing as well? Primary. Easy. Green, red & yellow. I got the majority of it right, lighting funereal processions with my Dollar Tree glow-in-the-dark rubber rings. The clerk told me that if I suck on them, they would sing. That grunting and whining, that isn't music, that isn't singing and I ain't sucking on nothing to see otherwise. Got my polish and my curtain repellent, spraying at it until it pulls away then shines up that pine box name plate so I can finally read it. Here's to infinity. Don't say no, baby, to a twin zero. Let's instead each duck our beings into its openings. A drug-addled industry begs for us to try. Try. Go for the one. The one that turned all of our joy into crushed credit card Seraphim. Duck your bill in and collect up the larvae. The eggs of Betty Wright's cleaning lady. In your veins, now in your grave. Come on baby, don't believe them when they throw at you ten questions and number nine is "Tell us something you've never told anyone else before."

Infinity.

Well, them kinds of things, they won't be yours for the publishing. Joshua tree Mormon buttoned hallucinogenics, we are listening. Hearing the crush of your every step and the only thing we was on then was chain lightning papering over the gilded streets with biodegradable 18 Wheelers, jack knifing the right side, hollowing out the newly opened entry. This piece here, the one we are removing, could be a song for the janitors and the urinal planetarium speed banks that are moving so quick that you could barely pick up the scent of nonbelief. When you find me, find me on my knees. On my knees most likely bowing from the weight of this backpack of unintended blues, this soda water in soft plastic, Frito Lay chipped aluminum siding that was attached later to keep the breath in and the hospiced ending at bay. You and I, that very Sunday, puzzled together all of the change that we had between the two of us, and well, we did in fact do something.

THE
EMBARRASSMENT
CORRUPTED DRIVE

MANY OF THE chapters in this book are about artists that are no longer among the living, or bands that have broken up. This speaks more to the timelessness of music than to the archaeological obsessive in me. There was no map or charted course, and even as I was in the throes of writing the chapter on Tim Buckley, The Fall and Billie Holiday inserted themselves. They were the last thing on my mind as I sat down with silence before me to write. This is a music less DJ session. This is me back at KSPC going in with no playlist and letting the leash of the headphone cord deliver me as far away from concrete thought or premeditated ideas of what that two-hour show would sound like. We get to do these things in our real lives, act on a whim, chase down a thought, meditate away the illusory before us to land somewhere we never thought to visit. We are anonymous, we are not broadcasting. We are living hard drives.

There is a library in one room of my house, and it spills out into the garage. Music, films, books; sure, those can be corrupted -destroyed by fire or flood, stolen or lost on loan, sold or given away. But living in a cloud or a stream or a database that holds, even for the almost unpossessive life of many of us, rootlessly, floating, beholden to ASCAP, BMI bean counters? Yuck. No thanks. These things slip away as well, publishing or legal rights, mechanical royalties unpaid, yanked from one platform and sent to another. A hard copy of *Woman In The Dunes* or *Cisco Pike*, films I may only watch one more time in my life, do I need them? Not right now. They serve as insulation to this home, both mentally and spiritually. I may need them again just as I need that pole pruner for the citrus trees. It is spending its life banging around the ladders in the garage, or all them extra chairs folded up in wait on those shelving units keeping that pruner company. Once, maybe twice a year, I take it out for a ride.

I am embarrassed by my wealth of choices down in that room and spilling into the garage. It is not a trophy room, it is a breathing thing that I am constantly checking volumes out of, I mean, daily. I am feeding it, at times too much. A slew of Roscoe Mitchell albums once, a thrift store find of UK press Echo & The Bunnymen 12″ singles, that promo only Big Dipper 12″ that includes a demo as well as a cover of Husker Du's "Girl Who Lives on Heaven Hill" that can only be found on side two. All of these came home with me in minute pieces, a collection built over four decades. These aren't coins or baseball cards or Spider-Man action figures that I had as a youth and discarded when I needed room. I was unattached to those things.

This collection isn't me, just as the house I am paying off isn't me. Hell, I know my children aren't me, something else to dote or live vicariously through. This virus I picked up, it is an obsession that even as I sit with it in the confines of middle age, has but a few cures. All or nothing for me; the house burns down; this collection won't be built back up again. No back up hard drive insurance. No safety copies tucked safely somewhere that I don't reside. You live under this roof, you gotta be vulnerable just like the cats and the kids and Catherine and the termite-dotted fascia boards. How many hundreds and hundreds of homes have I visited as a rag and bone man, buying collections. That trap, that is the trap that when this mortal coil shakes, I have already unwired safely. Then two kids that played drums and guitar and video games and trains and cards, they both will lay claim to it. I have helped to empty homes and move possessions belonging to far too many friends or family members of mine after they have passed away to have not addressed this issue. Like my pop, paranoid and making sure I knew where the key was to his safety deposit box and the address of the bank I would need to go to when he died (not "in the event" or "if," always the adult version of things even as a nine-year-old in his car) I have my living will lined out for them. Hey, they are nice guys, and I am sure there will be some records neither of them will want. Will they have the energy and time to throw my Tono-Bungay or Times New Viking records on to see if they will float through their lives as well? If you are into that shit, be in touch with them in 2050. I expect that my sentence here will ride me up to about then.

CARL REINER &
MEL BROOKS
THE 2045 YEAR OLD MAN

CHRIS BELL
EVEREST

FAREWELL. ONE OF THE WORST WORDS in the English language followed closely by forlorn. Stuck inside a phone booth casket without a dime; no proper way to say goodbye, to see you off. Carving into the glass with my keys after breaking off the teeth of one and the stem of another trying to jimmy the door, shards dancing around the upper most layers as I operated on that hardened sand, wiping away the dust of that first "I" that I carved in. Shit, shit, SHIT. This fucking hurts and this fucking sucks and my faculties are failing me now even as I try to compose this after the fact. Staring at a cursor, blinking back; these things are awful when they move laconically over months and years, when you have every opportunity to say and hear all that needs to be dredged up and properly buried. In a flash, and there is no goodbye, with its months and years of hangovers, of memory foam pushing the weight of the sea up and over you, you little rip tide, you little red riding knee high, you sniveling 8 pm bedsit idiot. All of those cancer sitcoms we watched with ill-prepared alien laughs. Laughs that we never got to spend fully. All of the silence that we tired out, awoken with heads against the wall, socks and shoes and lights all on. You were supposed to be here. You are supposed to be here right now with me. Cheap red plastic pails that the kids used at the beach, I am using now to keep the place from flooding. Holes in the roof, in the floor-boards; remember when you couldn't get out of bed? Well I can, and I can't right now. It is pathetic. It makes me feel even lesser. You at the family picnic when you were deep into it, and I can't even answer the door as my pal in his red Corolla drops some soup and salad and bread at my porch with a cardboard box razored at the gross discount club store. It was not just a fare thee well to you, it was farewell to us. With you no longer here, farewell to me. I take two knees, and I knock them and I attempt to stand up and do something. Every morning. Every morning. You think then, it was easy for those with sorrow that wasn't just a community college prop? With houses that served poorly as homes and an apartment that when my nephew walked in, said it felt like a cold set on loan. Here I am, apologizing on the phone, on the computer, on the stoop, in the shower. Forlorn. We don't get over anything. If we work at it, we get under it, and we view the roots of it, and we bend with the first few feet of mudded rain, then meld with the subterranean shadows; we know there is a way out of here, but that way is lost to us. That path is narrow and with our swollen bodies whose clothes no longer fit us, we can't, just now, be going.

It is safe to say now, things I only thought then. As old friends were put to sleep and out of their misery by methamphetamine, second story hangings or slow dance alcohol induced IV drippings. It is I that must speak for them now. I have to father uncle you. I have to appear even-keeled at processions and hear the generation beneath me confess to their suicidal longings. I keep my trap shut, I reveal next to nothing. Look at me, look at me without listening, and you will see it all. I am not trying to fool anyone, but I am acting. Acting. Jean-Paul Belmondo with no reservations—stoic. Stoic like Barbara Stanwyck's old west style, years after a scissor to the eye fury. It will get easier. You will have other losses. You will have real losses that will make those of your youth pale. It is my deepest hope and prayer that your long life will serve to comfort those that have either more or less than you. That even with your missteps and mistakes, they won't come to define you. That the salvation that you found early on does not create other sharp edges that come to haunt, then hurt you. You and I, pithy little insects attracted to flame in our shanty shack

Abbey. Paint all day, with their have you heard the good news blues leaking into the hallway, music, scripture rags, churches of our own making. Let's you and I, to the heavens send, a peal of bells that even the believers will understand. A couple of days after Christmas, I found your coat in the closet, you left here without it to see some kind of polar vortex. I should have known to look both ways for you before you crossed yourself.

EAST CLAREMONT
VILLAGE OTHER
ON ESP

IT IS NOT A CHARACTERISTIC that is exclusive to the American experience. The boot strings are pulled up in every other country as well. Go on and visit them or read about their history and the people that slogged through the most precarious of chapters in real time. We are able, as citizens of the world, to create in our mind even in the cases when that thought could be the cause of imprisonment or death. In better climes, we are allowed to jump into the deep end and do something that we don't know but maybe the first thing about, that, too, is a universal chord. You can only be naïve about any given thing once. Take advantage of that naïveté of youth, and should you be so lucky, old age it too. Joseph Campbell's arc is the same as the biblical one or the Grimm one. Obstacles in scripture or in fairy tales, those may serve as cheerleaders for some. Obstacles in the real world, those can be coaxed to be tales or myths, pushed down or out, or beaten in time by our actions. One small misstep can land on either side of things. Be the opposing equal to those tiny steps down the road of iniquity. At the risk of Alan Wattsing or Anthony Robbinsing you to death, look no further than the miracles of the last century. From unbelievable corners grew the most sublime of things.

Bernard Stollman, a lawyer by day whose clientele included musicians, was taken to an Albert Ayler gig in 1964. By the end of the set, the wheels were in motion for Stollman to start a record label so that he could release an album by Ayler. Stollman, who was a true believer in the idea of creating a universal language, Esperanto, and whose label was shorthand for that language, ESP, would go on to release the record *Ni Kantu En Esperanto* a sing-along record in Esperanto. The work of any publisher worth their weight is to bring art forth that would not see the light of day had they not the means to push forth works into the world that would at best sit latent, or worse, be lost. Although the tag line is that the artist alone decides what you will hear on their ESP release, which is not to say there weren't suggestions, which were merely that, in the case of records by Patty Waters or Albert Ayler. A lawyer, one who learns the language of legalese and Latin as a means to insert themselves into your life at your greatest time of need—for a fee most of the time—is a hard thing to trust. In his private life, I think Stollman worked pro bono, him as a patron of the arts to be made fun of and cordoned off into an easily-mocked underground. Mij the Yodeling Astrologer? Was this a punchline created to toughen him up as he readied releases by Octopus, Cromagnon, and The Har-You Percussion Group which were all released later that same year? He was just a few years away from putting out recordings by Billie Holiday and Charlie Parker, but they were sandwiched between records by Frank Lowe, The Godz and the comedic ragtime parody of The Captain Matchbox Whoopee Band. Never let them see where you are going and don't get ahead of your feet.

Gatekeepers and archeologists are not in much demand these days. The electric grid is used up by all them millions and millions of soapboxes and megaphones—weed through them at your peril. It isn't all that much different than the foresting that we used to do reading magazines, left of dial X-ray tuners, scouring used record stores to find the gems in the chaff. Old people, always trying to tell you either how much better things are today for you or how much better things were in the past before you. No one has that kind of exclusivity; there is no single method that works. Be mindful of what is quick and easy before you, omnipresent in broad daylight. I pushed the bar down on a drinking fountain at my old elementary school recently and got blood all over my shirt. Blood that must have been packed there tightly in the faucet by some prankster. I wondered if my newly-minted vampire bib was better or worse than what used to fly out of that thing at our then tiny faces. Faces so small, we could barely be seen.

HORACE TAPSCOTT
SESSIONS VOLUME 23

HIS FIRST INSTRUMENT was the trombone, maybe it was the cold metal that didn't speak to him, no J.J. Johnson would he be. Hear him on late fifties into early sixties Lionel Hampton recordings playing the unwieldy thing. His youth in Los Angeles was colored by his family's friendships with jazz greats Gerald Wilson and Buddy Collette before he moved on to playing with Lionel Hampton, Sonny Criss, and others. His Pan-African People's Orchestra not only displayed Tapscott's talent and activism, but was a method for him to reach out to younger players and mentor those in the LA jazz community. Those that championed him started record labels to release his music. Not one or two patrons of the arts, but three of them. Imagine that, a trinity starting up record labels from scratch to release your music. Tom Albach's Nimbus Records was founded in 1979 after Albach heard some unissued tapes of Tapscott. Albach had the foresight to record eleven records of Horace alone at the piano starting in the early '80s. *The Tapscott Sessions* are made up of recordings the label owner made of Tapscott cordoned off in what I imagine looks similar to some of the rooms at Thatcher Music Hall in the basement of Pomona College. These recordings are some of the most beautiful records ever made. On volume six in the series, his original "Ancestral Echoes" is a thirteen-minute meditation that captures at the heart of things what an incredible listener and player he was. All of his influences are here and as a bonus, you hear in his playing those that he surely influenced (from McCoy Tyner to Matthew Shipp). What Coltrane's classic quartet does so well, Tapscott matches in this solo piece that runs the gamut from that Johnny Hartman standards record of Trane's to "Interstellar Space." Is that Tapscott plucking strings inside the sternum of the piano à la Cage to make it sing like a harp near the coda of the song? What kind of magician is this that does not use smoke and mirrors, but breath and force?

I draw upon the piano that sits behind me as I write this. That piano is a Baldwin, Tapscott's was a Steinway. My pop couldn't afford a Steinway, but like the shanty house he first bought after the divorce, he saved up and moved house by house over decades to better ones on the rungs. His new pianos would arrive just like his new used cars—my brother, sister and I checking out every key or every car window, glove box, sustain pedal, defrost control. Before the divorce, I would sometimes hear him playing plaintively in the mornings or in the late eves. Later then, when the piano moved to his apartment, he would play in the evenings, on the weekends, alone, or when he hosted parties and was too shy to make it around the room. He would catch his second wife with that piano, playing I don't know what song on that Baldwin. Throw out a song title; he would knock it for you by ear. Not many recordings exist of him playing, but when I throw on a side of Horace Tapscott, we are both back at his house again, both of us listening closely. Maybe that is why I don't visit that graveyard in Riverside when I need to listen to my dad, or be with him. He is right there in front of me or beside me when I turn quick enough to see. Most of Tapscott's records are out of print right now and going for decent dollar on all them vulture sites. As I delve deeper and age ungracefully, his recordings speak deeper to me, reveal hidden bars that are odes to others. That same note comes to me from my pop as I recall things he said or did, those notes developing a different tone over my lifetime and the decades since his departure. My only regret is that there aren't more recordings of my two favorite pianists, but that is a minor thing, and I am thankful that it is such a minor thing in this world of major flats and sharps. Those that are gone are right here with us, some of them still playing and singing, listen as hard as you possibly can, bite down on the knuckle of your index finger if it gets more difficult still.

Yves Montand
Sings Scott Walker

E VE WAS EXTREME. She had always been. As a youth, she was obsessed with ballerinas. Her first Halloween tutu. Her posters of Nijinsky, Pavlova and the ubiquitous Baryshnikov were her Russian trinity hung with looped masking tape on the four back corners surrounding her bed from what she can remember her ten-year-old bedroom looking like then. Puberty and a pair of skates for her thirteenth birthday delivered her into the culture of roller skating. This wasn't just roller skating at the rink or down the street or at a park. This was roller skating as a way of life. Three solid years, say thirteen to sixteen, that time in life that is a lifetime unto itself with its long days and listless nights. That time spent imagining or doing the one thing that she loved above all else. With this love her talent blossomed, and in turn so did her collection of skates. Some pairs didn't deliver where others did, some given away to friends or flung in the back recesses of her closet over time, gathering a blanket of dust to keep themselves warm in that cold. Shopping for a new vehicle every other month or so, what a thrill. Riedell, Sure-Grips, Candy Rollers, Nash Cruisers, JC Higgins (white, leather), Free Forms, Hard Candy LT429s, and a myriad of variations in between. There were pairs that delivered advantages for different techniques, and depending on the day and dime, decisions would have to be made before choosing and lacing. Will there be more curb-ramming than Wile E. Coyote stops on Saturday? Tuesday evening, toe-drag spin outs out-numbering wind braking runs? Runouts, chop-stops, heel drag spin outs—where and with whom, solo, boardwalk, casual or hardcore. There was a pair and a purpose for every set in her collection.

It was a singer she would be for a flash, before she got into dance. An undergraduate program at the University of Iowa led to deeper schooling prior to her first paying gig as a backup dancer. Business consultants don't begin their journey to become business consultants, nor do choreographers. Being a choreographer for Eve was not her dream, but that was where she landed. She thought of the vocation as a synthesis of chemistry, nurse practitioner, doctor, confidante, student of muscle, bones and psychology— all of the talents she had to employ to gain the entry to a better heeled, circle moving clientele. At first it was the act of coming up with routines, flipping the clichés on their head, which in and of itself is a mean feat. She would imagine how a three-legged woman would run, a cheetah on an escalator, brainstorm as many ideas as she could, pausing here and there to pantomime that movement, first in her head, then in the mirror. She graduated to then having to create movement to study, movement that she could not employee another to do, so she did it herself. Tying her arms behind her back, soaping the floor and filming her falls; drying cement swan dives, hot coal leaps. Once these means were exhausted, she began thumbing through glossy catalogs, making high and low website purchases of compression wear, lumbar support, orthotics, S&M leather, rubber, uppers downers, and platforms. It was in one of these get ups that she first sprained her ankle as an adult. Her first thought then, was, what can I do with this? It wasn't as if she had to go to an ER to tend to the sprain. The sprain worked, gave her a right leg leap with a left leg drag that her largest client at the time thrilled to try at one of them teetering-on-bankruptcy award shows. It was no moonwalk, no chattering key next minute gratification, but those in the know knew, and some of them did seek out Eve.

More restrictions were needed to work new muscles, form new body language. It was this endless demand of new birth, the unseen visible for audiences by their clients, the performers. Have you ever purposely broken bones in your body? Certainly some have, maybe to get out of school or to file false charges against your spouse, but it is doubtful that anyone you know went to extremes such as having bone marrow replaced in their lower left leg, joints removed with carbon-coated implants for the sake of only creative movement. Know of anyone that asked their doctor friends about a fluid that would outperform the bodies organically made synovial solution? In her day dreams, a stream of bees replacing her ulna, IVs of saline that would target only her upper body with fluid such that the hips and legs would have to compensate. All of us in our vocations fall back on that which is natural or easy to us. That is the death of an artist. Good ones must always be reaching, and the sorrowful endings are the curtain calls of those that over arch. You ever seen a dancer's body at the end of their life? Compare them crooked ankle wrists, cartilage free knees and heel-less feet to those that have seen combat. "Give them a script, don't film it. Record a record, don't tour behind it. Paint all day; don't let a gallery owner see it. Keep your body, your heart, your soul, locked open on the outside. Make it visible. Let them see it. Every vein, every chamber, but don't let them run their blood into it," Eve would write years later in the introductory pamphlet for the Scott Walker Dance Academy.

X

SHE HAD TO LEAVE SAN DIMAS

I T CAN BE ARGUED, and I can possibly be sold, that there exists consecutive records by a band, starting with their debut release, as stellar as the first four X records. I do mean the first four records, not the middle years or the fluke of a mid-career renaissance. If I remove that stringent rule of it being the first four albums, there are others that have hit this milestone. Coltrane's classic line-up is one that comes through the ether to me immediately, without cheating. Coltrane was of course years in before he hit that stride, and better strides still after that stretch too. But what band (not singer/songwriter, much easier to have a vision than share and create a vision within a group) has an out-and-out fully formed debut record, followed by three equally fantastic records? Even with my disdain for nearly every Los Angeles scene post 1962 and my being unfairly suspect of dress up, the first four records by X are untouchable. X was like The Who, each member utterly unique and the least likely of friends, let alone a group. Whereas Moon and Entwistle were show-offs, Billy Zoom was stoic with that knowing smile, and DJ Bonebrake (the only California native in the band) slowly revealed his talents over the course of these four records (the footage of him in his kitchen in the documentary *The Unheard Music* is priceless, but if it was anyone else, I'd be hard-pressed to not think it was some showing-off of some latent jazz fusion rock chops). John Doe and Exene? Forget it man, those two voices, those lyrics, they are the grown-up version of what their producer Ray Manzarek was attempting to do with his man child in his band. Literate, edgy, economical musically and lyrically. If there is an after-life, theirs will be the voices that when I am led out of this world, will be singing to me.

Having seen X live with various line-ups for thirty plus years, I have never walked away from a show of theirs with the original line-up that was not revelatory or, at the very least, celebratory. This having missed those key shows tied to those first four records. I was present at one of the December 1987 recordings of what came to be their *Live at the Whisky a Go-Go* double LP. Tony Gilkyson on guitar, a pregnant Exene on vocals. I bought the record when it came out, sold it off some years later and have not replaced it since. I underline that only to clear the air that I am not nostalgic about this opinion, stuck living in a loop of the past. Hell, I was eleven when *Los Angeles* was released, and though I recall for some reason being aware of other Southern California punk bands whose records I had seen at Licorice Pizza (The Dickies), logos spray painted on the rocks of Mount Baldy (Black Flag) or cousins kicking names, cassettes around (Surf Punks, Agent Orange), X came into my life when a used copy of *More Fun In The New World* priced at $4.99 turned up at the record store a week or two after its release. To the point of the power of the original quartet, bless his heart, the band with Tony Gilkyson is a totally different band. I was reminded of how different when Billy Zoom was too sick with cancer to play a show four or five years back and a substitute guitarist filled in for him. It just wasn't there. Yet, even when I scored a free ticket to see them live at The Forum opening for Pearl Jam in July of 1998 (the original quartet), they killed. They killed in one of the worst venues in Southern California even from my cheap seat view. I can't recall any of the shows at The Forum that I have seen over the years making much of an impression on me (excepting that Kiss show in 1978 with Cheap Trick opening, I was nine, give the kid a break). Bob Dylan with Tom Petty, sucked there. Roger Waters touring his first solo album with blowhard Eric Clapton on guitar 1985, doubly sucked. I am panting as I write this, trying to squeeze in every angle of this argument to make sure that I have sold you on this, but then, who cares? I have four spare copies of them first four X records tucked away for safe keeping. It may not be a desert island where I am going, probably some chain restaurant that I'll be celebrating some arms-length birthday for a decade, so I'll need some company there that speaks to my kind of hell.

SWANS
FRESH

O THER ACTORS, OTHER PUNK ROCKERS, they chose for themselves names that would represent their new mindsets. You, kicked around and kicked out, hitchhiking on LSD, chose for yourself something graceful and beautiful, and you did in fact become that. Announcing who you were at the onset of it all, in a different language, one that you were raised with and had to be exorcised out from you. Pianos down the stairs. Vials of mercury floating in the backed-up side of the sink that housed the garbage disposal. What did you think would happen? Anyone could see the answer to that riddle from four thousand Popsicle sticks away. Your two worlds started to reveal themselves on separate sides of the dead wax tracks. Just when the underground world at large had you pegged, you swung drastically to the far extreme. That major label debut and your show in Hollywood at The Palace, where I was one of maybe a few hundred in that one fifth filled club. Your set started on the somber note of "I Remember Who You Are" as some kind of riddle for the audience that was there to try to open up to their old favorite band, now wrapped up in a Blind Faith cover and a Mapplethorpe sheet. We are put to bed and shamed endlessly for what we do that does not come easy to us, strange offshoots and failures. Lemon tree sucker shoots, their limbs reaching from up under that cambium layer. These are still acts of ambition, and so too, you. The decade to follow would offer hundreds of variations on the theme of The Swans, but would not be Swans records. Flick that garbage disposal switch; watch what water and electricity and mercury become when they are finely mixed into one. Everything that was there before was present then in the '90s through the double aughts. Some would say that these recordings are missing the musical savagery of your youth, but often by those that haven't survived through savagery.

I don't want to see you wounded again. Don't want you to return to that desk or to your youthful lashes. I dig your post free jazz Pablo releases with that octave lowered-by-age voice. Show me all of your wrinkles, show me your age, your age, like you do with the best of your work. That's right kiddies, this prosthetic and this cane; these are what adorn us as we make our way to the end. Don't sugar up or omit, don't leave out any of the details or try to hide the script. I came here to see you now, to hear you as you now are. No one behind the cigarette-holed curtain hitting the heights for you, no, go wrong, it is OK. You are with those that love you. You are with an audience that will forgive nearly anything. A member of the audience, after befriending me and chatting through the opening act rolls up her shirt sleeve "Did I tell you about this fresh bruise on my forearm? That one I must have gotten in my sleep. I didn't feel a thing."

YOKO ONO
FLY 2

WE WERE AT THAT YOKO SHOW at The Orpheum in LA when you chewed up your ticket stub and stuck the bits in my 2 ears because it was so loud then and you brought to me something then, so sweet. Is there nothing here that I can do that would mean as much to you? You could just stand here by me. No need to be like Superman. Don't you Supertramp me and reverse the spin. Turn time around, turn time to now, right now, you and me. If you would just stand here with me, we could chance our two futures together. We could. Let's chance them both, darling, bend them together until they bleed into one solid line, you and me.

Our new favorite song, it is called "Fly." Fly too, fly 2, fly to the moon, to the moon and back again. There are other songs that she sings. There is "Dub Train" and much later, the glorious "Will I" that she recorded with her son. The world-at-large wasn't ready for her then, they are never ready in their coliseums and arenas for much other than football and lion maulings. "I could do that," you could hear them sneer at any Sears or Zodys, any Gemco as they pick through what is before them, pulling it in close to make it their own. I don't dig Frank Stella nor Jeff Koons or Damien Hirst mind you, but their work doesn't send me into a racist, misogynistic screed. Performance can serve as an installation. Yoko cutting away at her dress or her and her husband's bed in performance twelve hours a day at the Hilton Amsterdam; this was their honeymoon. Al Capp, creator of the Li'l Abner comic strip, visiting the couple to voice his grievances, a second rate unfunny cartoonist, trying to unbutton her in bed, in bed then with her husband, on the world stage. "Good God, you've gotta live with that," he says to Lennon before telling the two of them, "Whatever race you're the representative of, I ain't a part of it." Imagine that, traveling all that way to say such things. What kind of strength did she have then you might ask? Or was this all art by provocation, meant to elicit reactions as any work does?

She would be the butt of jokes for decades. She was the talisman touchstone that broke up the band. There she was, ridiculed on a world stage as that band used the last of its strength to put itself to bed reasonably. I would argue that the greatest feat by The Beatles was a collaboration with Yoko. None of them get credit for two of their finest works—assimilation and divorce. When others joke about someone or other being the Yoko of the band, I wonder if they mean an artist of force and vision brought to the table, to push and question, to bring a different perspective and other colors to the palette. A Japanese Woman in a British skiffle band. And though not her doing, as the members of the band have reflected on thousands of times since, had there been a separation as gargantuan in the music world before the Beatles split? A divorce that, like their records, ushered in a new era, new places to go to for many of their listeners as the '70s dawned. Pining for reunions, superglued together solo tracks to try to imagine what might have come next.

Yoko was the Jackie Robinson of the band, the graceful one that did not let the weight of sexism and racism crush her; did not let all of the negativity that was left at her door daily color her outlook, which managed to remain as positive as could be expected of anyone during the most trying of times. There would be an interview just a day before he was assassinated. He, and her, and I paraphrase; discussed how there was too much thought and speculation and fantasy about hatred and wars. *Star Wars*, one of them said, couldn't those movies have been called *Star Peace*? And her? Unfl,nching grace married to a "fuck you, don't look at me." There would be one of the most beautiful ballads of the 20th century, "Goodbye Sadness," that she would write and record for 1981's *Seasons of Glass*. A few years later, she made *Star Peace* a reality—a crap record, but a reality nonetheless. Every artist needs a nadir. Her Beatles cohorts weren't exactly hitting home runs or even singles then with Paul's *Give My Regards To Broad Street*, Ringo's *Old Wave,* & George's *Gone Troppo* hitting at approximately the same time. Slimy ass Alan Freed? Sexual predator Billy Preston? Kenny Rogers and America producer George Martin? Will the real fifth Beatles please stand up? Stand up, you witch, and fly.

HELDON
AURAL IMPLORER

S O MANY OF THE ELECTRONIC MUSIC pioneers of the '70s, second tier followers and bottom drawers of only wires, buttons and cheap knock-off adhesive tape, offer photos of themselves in front of their gear somewhere within the packaging of their release. Sure, Leo Theremin and the folks that utilized his theremin were photographed ad infinitum in front of the machine that he created, but artists like Morton Subotnick, Delia Derbyshire, David Tudor, and Pauline Oliveros, for the most part, were not part of this scrapbooking crowd. Even so, this kind of braggadocio is charming to me in ways that almost any other is not. Middle-aged men in front of their sports cars, parents hugging their newborn, graduated attorneys-to-be, social posts of some idiot's huge carbon footprint meal that is going to be trapped in that shell of a body that should not be photographed and later slide out as merde. I'll give, perhaps the attorney will work pro bono (we speak in Latin together, the attorneys and I). What the electronic musician is communicating when they are in front of their gear is not how large their vulva is, but almost a thank you card to the robotics and technology that made it possible for digits of the snapped artist to toil and come up with sound that then was fairly new to the world, and even now, just 50 years in, is still fetal. It is more akin to a picture of a newborn, sure, you made it, but without much effort. Thank you baby, I couldn't have done it without you. Heldon "IV" on the Aural Explorer label from 1976 marries these images together. A baby hooked up to all sorts of wiry umbilical cords that the listener can surmise are tied in to the equipment that Heldon member Richard Pinhas is photographed at the foreground of on the back cover.

France's Richard Pinhas was the heart of Heldon and would go on to record a number of records after he outgrew the umbrella of that name. He is a direct line between Brian Eno and John Carpenter, with his electronic tinfoil footprint pats and distorted mini Moogs, mellotrons, and synthesizers. Carpenter would boil down what Pinhas did for the sake of drama; Eno, well you know what he did. Pinhas's guitar playing, much of it built on sustained notes early on, would branch out over the post Heldon/ post heroin addiction years. He would go on to collaborate with Merzbow and a member of the Japanese band Ruins, bridging the divide between otherworldly atmospherics and the Eli Whitney on steroids mechanical guitar noise of this world. There is always a field of space before us, I move my hands through it trying to see further ahead but usually for as far as I can see, it is just some idiot in a crosswalk that can't even see their reflection on their phone as they stare down vacantly.

GLENN GOULD
THE CHAPLIN VARIATIONS

T HERE ARE ALWAYS UNUSUAL REQUESTS. An
artist that brings his tattered bench to every performance,
the rubbing of hands on a tree stump for luck, the insistence that
no red gels be put on any of the stage lights. We had acquiesced
to nearly every last one, in our home, every asterisk, every time.
Sometimes the far and away went unnoticed, untouched except by
the sycophantic entourage, or worse yet, left like a still painting
whose only redemption was that, were it food, it could go home
with the interns and pages. Is that what all of this work we were
doing was for? Show. Just for show. This lead up to the Sunday
performance was no odder than others we had fielded over the
last few decades. There was an insistence that the piano be lifted
ninety degrees such that the keys would be five foot four inches
from the stage. A Rube Goldberg device of I-beams dressed in
sashes where the metal met the Steinway was to be built on spec
by our in-house designers should we still want this performance
on our stage. This was months after the house had been sold out
and the contracts had been triplicate signed. Didn't we already
have a deal? Sure, but no deal is sealed. Sickness can be feigned,
there was that kid whose stomach was pumped of pop rocks and
jewelry, nearly his entire savings, which was still not to be believed
even all these years post '78. The kid never played. Go on ahead,
sue me, his ma said. The request before us was no stranger than
anything else that we had agreed upon for the sake of a performance. You want to remain in this business? Awash in a shower
somedays and some others, well, get in line & ready yourself to
be taken.

The afternoon of the performance saw our piano in the jaws of a drywall-less shark, up there on our stage, hooked and ready. A microphone resting in the cup of a six foot mic stand, boomless, straight. The base of the piano on one of those dreadful Crosby, Stills & Nash nylon knock-off Persian rugs. It was all we had, there were no directives in writing for a particular rug. My son jokes, you get the vomitorium rug that is what this rug is made for. This going to be some Nigel Kennedy bullshit firework display to make up for the lack of inspiration? Well, better that than one of them blue plate blank Marsalis pre estate sales. I had been a water boy; my kids had been gofers, my family & friends fetchers of non-necessity for years. None of this fazed any of us. Not the ten-year-old or his sixteen-year-old niece, not our sister or twenty-one-year-old soundman we got on the cheap, not the librarian nor the Libra photographer that kept our poster boxes unique. Go on ahead; I always give up my seat. Show me what you can do. Show me what you can do.

From rags to romance novels in the daily's. Ain't she lonely? Doesn't it get tiring? Them Victorian women redressing six, maybe seven times a day. Well, they didn't have to do all of the dressing and the pressing and the mending. Were they lonely in their gilded cage? You bet. She had a joke that was left on her husband's machine that morning. At my funeral, can you play "Dude Looks Like a Lady"? That or "Happy Birthday To Me"? Self-parked in the back alley, next to the Pittsburgh/Thai fusion cuisine take-out grease, parks her Geo, grabs her bags. A carry-on and a non-descript purse, maybe a prescription or maybe not a prescription, rattling as into the venue she makes her way. No manager, no agent, no accountant, just her and some sheet music. And one of those motherfucking tiny dogs that barely eats. What am I supposed to do in the presence of one of them? Smile, ask the rodent's name? Look at me, you can read me like a zine—easy, quick and cheap. A green room of enamel white-painted brick, white linen over an eighteen-year-old six by two table that has been knee deep in so much shit that someone with the proper authority would christen it a saint for all that it has been through. All yours for the afternoon, the evening, and the late night cheers or tears until we call up the security bars.

Up he goes, dream, come, dream, come, come, dream, dream come, come. He tears in with a B flat into a C major. At first, just the pounding, attack of the strings. Excited, they are making the other keys sound, the ones that have yet to be hit. A chorus of approval from the high E when the low E sounds. The walls are pulsing. Blue vein temple sensating. You could close your eyes then, you should have. You can see it better with your ears. Gates up and open? From the first dozen or so rows you could soon then easily see bits of fingernails flying in the mothen spotlight. I thought guitarists and pianists kept their fingernails cut close to the quick then, at least the left hand if you were a righty in the case of guitar, and I had never seen opaque fingernails a few inches long on the keys. More flecks of dust and skin in the nightclub limes, was it dirt carved off the keys, a trick then like water on a snare, glitter on a tom? Entire keys were carved from the instrument, digging in deep to the lower intestines, the mid-range down to the knee of the bass. Tendons pulled from a wax encasing. Little deadly asps crawling in the air, stilled on the ground, unwinding. Lifted, lifted, becoming, lifted, lifted until nothing was landing no more. Call off tomorrow, the bailiff booms. No need for any more exhibits or excuses or rings of keys. A bed of light, I have been blessed with this eve. The pianist steals a bow, and then goes back to work cutting the last of the teeth from the jaw of the grand. This is what I am paid so handsomely to do.

SHORT DOGS GROW
HOFFY

MID-EIGHTIES TOM WAITS, Matt Dillon, Twin/ Tone, Bostonian band Sorry! Yes, Sorry with an exclamation point. Your friend has a band, everybody's friend has a band, and they are all playing tonight. On the way to the dive, you ratatat on and on about Dorothy Stratten and director Peter Bogdanovich; Bob Fosse's film *Star 80* blurring into your Ben Vereen routine. Post teen blues blooming into something altogether different. We don't have any stage clothes; we barely have what you would call a wardrobe. It is short, and sweet, cuz none of us have much time or much money. Sure, this entire year may be in vain, won't stand for the ages, but we weren't building it to withstand time. There would have been more, but I was late getting up and had to hightail it to work when dawn started to spark through the windows, I had to go, I needed to clock in.

GLASS EYE
SMALLER

AUSTIN TEXAS' GLASS EYE were one of those idio-syncratic strange amalgamations of a band that comes only from members whose taste in music varies to such a large extent that it is incredible that the marriage of the four of them lasted for as long as it did. Progressive rock leanings, Henry Kaiser sharpened guitar leads, Linda Thompson vocal overlays, and Mick Karn fretless bass; how in the world could this band find common ground? Who in the world could like this band? There was a buzz in their hometown, and for good reason. No one in the world sounds like Glass Eye which, even in the case of bands that I detest, is something to be proud of. Female/male vocal tradeoffs by Brian Beattie and K. McCarty, both talented song-writers, painted onto an already dense and overcrowded canvas for some. McCarty would gain notoriety for a record of Daniel Johnston covers years later (she had championed him early on, having Daniel open for Glass Eye as possibly one of his first live performances). Beattie had played in legendary San Francisco punk bands Fang and Tapeworm (both featuring Tom Flynn who went on to helm the Boner record label, home of the early Melvins and Ed Hall who Beattie went on to produce along with other bands, mainly bands from Texas).

Local promoter Pat Bacich promoted shows in the surrounding area that I grew up in. Toppers in La Verne hosted Jane's Addiction; The Timbers in San Dimas saw the Southern California debut of ex-Hanoi Rocks members Andy McCoy and Nasty Suicide's Cherry Bombz. Dinosaur Jr, The Meat Puppets, Firehose, Soul Asylum and others played at Montclair's Green Door club.

Located across the street from the largest mall in the Inland Empire at the time, The Montclair Plaza, the club is long gone, replaced by a McDonald's and a clothing store named Phallus, which is such an incredible punchline that although I pass it a few times a week, I still manager to laugh alone on the driver side at least one in three passes. You may be holding onto your Tom Sawyer and Holly Hobby inner child, not sure that I have one of those, but if I do, he likes snickering and snorting so loudly that his "Ma, buying some suspenders at Phallus, will see you for dinner in a bit" is nearly unintelligible. Pat's "Bacich Presents" was ambitious, and today I barely fault him for his pay-to-play line-ups that were built into his Montclair booking; barely, but still. Booking shows is certainly one of the rings in Dante's hell. Seldom is anyone in the realm satisfied. The handshake is worse than any drug transaction or hooking you are likely to do. Coming or going, taking or receiving, you are cheapened for even playing. Poor Pat, seeking advice about booking Glass Eye, local musician and producer Rob DeChaine told him the band was not only fantastic, but they would be a huge draw in Montclair on what I recall as a weeknight. I think there were 8 of us at the show that night, but the band was on fire and I hope that they were able to claim a decent guarantee.

APHEX TWIN
DRUNQS

AFTER THE QUAKE OF PRINCE'S DEATH, there were inevitable aftershocks. Sure, the drugs and the last days, those sad pictures of him on his bike outside that pharmacy. The previously unpublished interviews, one of them detailing the dog-eared furniture and general run down fever at Paisley Park studios. For some of us, the most difficult thing to digest about Prince's death (not the drugs, that dancer's body took so much abuse in them high heels and them jumps that must have turned his heels and hips to mush) was the absence of a will or last testament. How could one so obsessed with control over his music, image and publishing not secure these facets of his legacy? Aretha Franklin, James Brown, Bob Marley, Barry White. None of them left wills and they were long enough in the tooth, and in the case of two of them, aware of their cancer diagnosis long enough in advance to at least scrawl some H&R version of their wishes. Why would they not leave a will? In Aretha's case, there have been three scrawled wills located as this goes to press, including the most recent one in a spiral notebook found tucked under a seat cushion. Did they want to avoid Jerry Lewising their legacy with a poisoned last testament leaving nothing for their kids? Think that death was far off, or in denial about shaking off their coil? Was it the lack of confidence in the legal system, the racism that permeates every last corner of it dating back to slaves signing with an X, contracts that took advantage of any non-silver spooned heel?

Sure, there was Sonny Bono, John Denver and a slew of younger artists that were not African American who died without leaving a will or last testament, but Sonny Bono was no Marvin Gaye, and John Denver a Billie Holiday he does not come close to. These were artists that fought for their artistry, worked for both social justice and the rights of musicians and writers, fought to have their voices heard but went mute when it came to protecting the trappings of the physical world for their family, and in some cases their legacy, there was not time or thought to do such. Bob Marley shampoo, Jimi Hendrix Coke v. Pepsi commercials, Prince credit cards and other scourges that surely these artists would not have rubber stamped, that now litter the digital landscape and $.99 store shelves.

You want to be on TV? We'll put you on the Jimmy Kimmel stage that is beholden to companies that manufacture razors with razor blade handles, antiseptics, sugar water tattoo blues... get up there and sing your song. Sign off on this for broadcasting. Sign this so we can own your performance. Richard James, at some horrid festival, arguing with a promoter, refusing to dance along. Being chased around backstage up to performance time, you will not go on until you sign. A big sharpie X on the contract. The promoter didn't even know what that meant, was only wondering if this was his real signature, if it would hold up in a court of law where he said he would sue the promoter for this deed. Is it any wonder why so many that don't die from the disease of showbiz, disappear? James came back, but at arm's length. No pharmacy, no Jimmy Fallon hair gel hip shakes. No free drink ticket sound check presented by cancer causing talc powder. X, former, no Os.

Donny Hathaway & Karen Dalton

Duets

MONEY WON'T CHANGE YOU. Ray Charles couldn't change you. Aretha Franklin couldn't, two gospel records in, change you. We aren't even counting the Curtis Mayfield cover—that we aren't counting. Dead in a rented room, if that is your destiny, well it comes quick and easy. It was Sam Moore who had to go on singing, after the coke and speed was long gone. Are you, too, going to leave us this way? Ah, no, please, Donny Hathaway from an Essex hotel. Ah, and then AIDS, in 1993, took Karen Dalton from her Woodstock, New York mobile home. She, she should have been travelling, what with that voice, guitar on her back. I imagine the two of them dueting, holy shit, Roberta Flack standing back and Tom Paxton on his knees. All of the anguish and mental illness that, in our real lives has inflicted itself upon the simple act of paying the bills or raising our children, what if again, it could be asked to and it did then, retreat, think of all that we could have. Her father in the upstairs apartment can't remember his name; and her kid, out off of Kingsley and Holt, he sold off what little he had left of himself. If you had a dollar, and I had a dime, I wonder would you borrow what little I had for the sake of staying alive. She sang that she needed less water than you would think. But they always claim, that were you to set them free, that they in turn would untether your needs. Let them fly away, find it in their hearts to staple wings to the proceedings, oh baby, but that isn't theirs to do. Sing. Sing. Using their trappings. The cell that grew up around the well when we were all thirsting; them stumble beginnings, they won't leave, they have the propensity to haunt you if you don't outgrow them. Is it in here that we have to makeshift percussion, rubber band orchestration? You wouldn't be able to believe it, sung by the third-string back-up singers. The ones too shy for the lime. Here we are, uncut, whole on your line.

All of the sorrow that mental illness and physical maladies have laid as waste upon our doorstep, well I, I swear I would take your share. I would background sing so you wouldn't have to do another session. Another uncredited confession; while some Brit white man, well, he sings your lead. Grooving. A Little Help From My Friends. Just as soon, doing what we two like to do. You and I, on our cheap little mattress, sweating out July. Are you, am I, going to come here only to leave you be in this rented room with nobody? Nobody to call on your GO phone. No one to cry to out the wrought-ironed window to. We together were both wondering. We gonna be as alien and inanimate as these surroundings? You, me, us are one. Will they recognize us? Will they let us through the door? The temperature is changing. The locks have new handshakes that I am trying to memorize as I wait here on the line. Fist, then thumb kiss, then high five? Four finger shake, right arm shoulder wrap then left? The combinations are endless, and I forgot which one they told me today to take. How about I just act like I used to do? How about when you see me in this state, you please, just act like you used to.

THE FLAT WORMS
KAREN CARPENTER
MEDICAL EMERGENCY

I T WAS AS IF THE CITY had planned to house the death of Karen Carpenter even when death seemed so far off for her. There in the upstairs of the home that Karen and Richard bought for their parents is where she lived out her last days. There is the gatefold sleeve of *Now & Then* from 1973 with the two of them driving by/away from the house in Richard's newly purchased 1973 red Ferrari. Rainy days and Mondays, double bummer, look closely at the cover, neither of them is smiling. Let's christen this town Downey, is there a pillar of the community that we can say we named the place after? Former Governor John Downey, the one that voted against his monied supporters on a bill that would put the prime strip of waterfront land into the hands of private companies, how about we name it after him? This is the kind of hope that is beaten down easily by detractors. It is a fight every day to hold onto your moral compass, and most of us don't have wolves at the door running for our seat or journalists offering pointers on weight loss or book of damnation balancing on your head grace walks. There is that sadness, but also a lift in the music that has sprung from Downey, California. Work your way through the canon of songs by the most noted musical siblings of the place— The Carpenters and Dave and Phil Alvin—to hear both sides of this conversation. Sure, metaldom's hometown act Dark Angel's seminal *Darkness Descends* includes "Death is Certain (Life Is Not)," "Hunger of The Undead" and "Merciless Death," so maybe theirs is a world with nary one pair of rose tints. Dig Dark Angel for running circles around the forever overreach of Elvis

Costello. Could he employ the following words, as Dark Angel do on the title cut of this record, in one song?: Peroration, servile, sacrosanct, abrogation, enmity, Stygian, inimical, ensanguined, mephitic and denouement? The clock is ticking Mr. McManus, get to work with Bacharach or McCartney STAT. The city's DJ Irene put together beats of edge-of-millennial electronica (oh, so nice that those of us who live in Los Angeles no longer have to hear that term daily on one of KCRW's always to be counted on, middle of the road DJ sets) and The Chantay's surf classic "Pipeline," was born here. Now, these upbeat songs to make up for the sorrow and end time library of Dark Angel only bring me down.

Like any home or city, there is a divide in taste and what grows in those places. Hoyt Stoddard Curtin and his scores are a large part of the fun found in the Hanna-Barbera musical canon— no sadness, a limited vocabulary, and just cartoon fun. Hoyt Stoddard Curtin was the Raymond Scott of Hanna-Barbera (*Flintstones*, *The Jetsons*, *Josie & The Pussycats*—were he alive today he would probably have an 8-track-only release on Burger with the brothers from Further/whatever their Eagles-inspired band was named, backing him up). Curtin also created the score for Ed Wood's *Jailbait* and the *C.H.O.M.P.S.* score. You might recall *C.H.O.M.P.S.*, a film made up of a nightmare panel from *Match Game* on display in their Monday's best—Wesley Eure (of the *Land of The Lost* Hanna-Barbera Saturday morning kiddie show), Red Buttons, Jim Backus, Valerie Bertinelli and of course the robotic dog playing the title role.

I doubt that Downey has a plaque on the former home of Hoyt Stoddard Curtin, or DJ Irene's apartment or the garage that Dark Angel got their start in, but that house that the Carpenter siblings bought their folks is a treasured landmark in Downey. There is no yellow sign on the lawn reading "Drive like your kids live here" or any of the other obvious markings of modern day suburbia that would just make you all the more sadder were you to pass it by.

Karen wasn't the kind of artist that needed those kinds of easy tropes. She could make a sci-fi themed song sad, a Beatles song morose and a Bonnie Bramlett & Leon Russell cut iconic. If you in fact drive by the house, do drive slow, and please don't stare, people that are well-loved once lived there.

DAVID RUFFIN
TRAGEDY AVERTED

IN ALL OF HIS RECORDS, built right in and sometimes around the sweetness and light, is heartache. Even his biggest hit with The Temptations, "My Girl," one of his imagined most joyous of vocals belies that very happiness. Is there a sadder Top 10 song whose lyrics are as upbeat as "My Girl"? Sure, there are contenders, but listen to "My Girl" again and push them second tiers down the rungs. David Ruffin. His vocals like the writing of Hank Williams or Hemingway. Emotion tucked into every shadow, hiding beneath the beat. Ruffin is one of those rarified artists that can employ the very weakness of a song—or a song's perceived overproduction—to the greater good of the tune. Hunh? "I'm Just A Mortal Man" written like most every song on his self-titled record by Bobby Miller, has a vocal that speaks so brutally and honestly to Miller's lyrics, that the syrupy backing vocals are forgiven, a clarion of falsehoods put in place to spotlight Ruffin's true to you pain. Check out, from his 1974 LP *Me 'N Rock 'N Roll Are Here to Stay*, Norman Whitfield's penned "I Saw You When You Met Her." An incredible example of him ripping past what most couldn't. Wind & rain, strings, phased instruments—a song some have called a claustrophobic, overly-dressed mess. Maybe those Jann Wenner listless listeners couldn't see past Whitfield's ambitious production. Maybe I have to use this middle-aged torso to fuck to death the undying corpse of *Rolling Stone* magazine so hard that it finds its proper perch beneath the alkaline of the Salton Sea. This seven-minute epic has always played to the ear like a man pushing aside every hurdle, every phony sweetener put in his way, to get to the nitty gritty truth. Heartbreaking, nearly every last song he sang. He was the unsanded plank at the Motown finishing school. Go on ahead, wipe your feet on him, and take him for granted. Put that torso to rest young man, I nearly hear Ruffin spotlight shaming me, "You are doing it all wrong, son."

THROWN AWAY

for the second time
was it good for you?
as good as the first time?
you an insect flying every place
but no home wants you
they screen out all your calls
and they burn the couch you slept on
and they pray for weakened signs of you
the same way that we then pined for your return
come home now
please
my sweet throw away
even that,
that was an attempt made
your throw away

you called us in to see Halloween
you bent the will of Thanksgiving
and now you think surrender is December's way?
when you already surrendered everything
is that when they finally get you under the hot lights?
trying to put a warmed-over McDonald smile on your old new
    self, then?

We hadn't the wealth to keep the heat on all night
we huddled and we threw blankets on our pyre
we didn't think it would light so soon
so soon

strike one
strike two
do you really need me at your hard luck ball?
won't you please come
won't you please come to mine?

strike three
thrown away
not a bar
not a refrain
no man made home could hold you
hold you
hold you like thrill held you
hold you like jail held you
held you like all that they imported in
from emirates and high stake whims
to strike you out
to strike you down
to get you curbside
thrown away

GUY CLARK
THE SHRIMPERS AND
THEIR LADIES

I MISS THEM ALL. Hoyt Axton, David Blue, Mickey Newbury, Linda Bruner. There is a concrete step just above them and a splintering handrail to the immediate left, as fluid as these kind of things are and some days any one of us can float above the fray. A morning in Omaha listening to Axton's *My Griffin Is Gone* while Sara shuffles in the kitchen and Fante gets close enough to pet without growling, that turned out to be one of them perfect days that, upon returning to California, made me dig out my copy, play it, be thankful for the foresight at having picked it up years ago and foresight to pack it with me for every move. "Motley Mary Ann" recorded in 1967 by Chicago's Pisces ended up on a mix tape from a friend years ago prior to Numero issuing an entire record of theirs that had never seen the light of day until 2009. Pisces featured Linda Bruner on vocals and a band in front and behind her that delivers even forty years past the expiration date. Old friends, some we could not know until they were gone.

I have not listened to the final Guy Clark record. I haven't been able to bring myself to break the seal of the plastic wrapped heartbreaking cover. This is outside of my nature. When I die, you won't find many books in my house that, even if I didn't make it through, I hadn't at least cracked the spine of and gotten somewhere with them. Records? When I buy them, they get opened fairly quickly and nothing gets filed into the ocean of vinyl or aluminum until it has been listened to a few times. Forgive the overflow of a hundred records when you visit me, I have not yet digested them and I don't want them to get lost at sea. Oftentimes as I am writing this book, I am so sorry that it is a one way conversation and that I am inserting myself in places where instead I wish you and I were having a conversation. I have always been a better listener than reader, writer or viewer. But even then, there are some things I can't brace myself to read or to watch or to hear in the present. I am trying to prepare and preparation is a fool's game. Here is the last novel by your favorite author. The half way finished film that friends rallied around to complete when that director fell ill suddenly, the table scraps cobbled together for a compilation, the thematic spines that match the newly reissued entire works. Hell, even the half scribbled notes of a painter whose work spoke to you before you were teenaged has the weight enough to stop you half cold.

My Favorite Picture Of You is Guy Clark's final record. There stands Clark stoic on the cover, holding a Polaroid picture of what a friend told me is his wife of over forty years, Susanna. Susanna who had recently passed on when this picture of him with that image in hand was taken, holding it there, as proof. Imploring you, this is what love is, this is the gold vein I mined during the entirety of my life and at the end of mine, I am going to push this into the foreground, let it obscure me. Susanna in color, arms folded, post-fight? Post coital? On the porch, maybe en route to Tastee-Freez, maybe on the way into that 1950's Texas bungalow. We are older, so these things have the wherewithal to deeply affect us. Sure, we had lost friends in our early twenties, but now well into middle age we have lost plurals and plurals of family and friends. They haunt us. They remind us. They keep us honest in their absence. Guy Clark's final record has one of the most touching record covers you will ever see. There it has been for a few years, standing out from the bulk of this wasted lifetime of collecting, whispering, "I am not ready for that Neptune landing yet."

ERNEST TUBB
...OF BLOOD

2 AM UPLAND REHAB CENTER. I had fallen asleep in one of them uncomfortable chairs that they make specifically for these facilities. They are usually up against a wall, directly across from the bed. Daring you to sit down and look on, dead on. These chairs, they are manufactured for both the eye and the body, manufactured to be uninviting. You have to move the things and place them bedside where they are meant to look askew, if only slightly out of place, as you hold his hand. "Please, don't stay long" they begin. Then, later into the night maybe, "get the fuck out and let us do our job without your insolent critical eye." Months previous to tonight he had said he might take my advice, but I am sure he had said that to his sister and his mother and his other friends and his ex-wife prior to me. We would go eat at Vince's, a middle-class treat we called it, bring something home to his mom. Don't add a 20% tip to the food we are taking to her, he would tell me, we are serving her, not them. Two weeks from Vince's he had me help him get gas in the car, at a specific gas station, not an Arco or a Thrifty, but the one that he had come to the conclusion had the highest quality fuel at the best price. His stomach taking on water then, he needed help getting out of the car. A few days later he landed here. A crew of his best friends circle each other, try to secure each night. Try to, if you can, secure the nights. The best advice I can give anyone is to never let a loved one out of your sight when they are in any kind of facility. Think about the fast food fuckery that happens with your dropped tile meat; apply that to your health in a hospital ward, a waiting room, any outpatient inn. IV bags left on the bed, the wrong meds given, the lack of attention, the near everything they have to offer, demands attention and watchfulness. Try not to get over exhausted. Find some family and friends you can rely on that are capable to tend to these things.

That second week in, you fell asleep first, I started to read then awoke in a start with a sweaty chin on my neck, 2am. It was Ben Vereen, on TV—*Pippin*. The room was darkened, and the remote nowhere to be found. I was sitting with you and Ben Vereen, and all I could think about was them scenes from *All That Jazz*. What a fucked little world this is. You and I are huge fans of music and cinema. We both hate musicals. (We came up with two between us one night that we liked—*The Blues Brothers* and *Une Femme est Une Femme*.) So here you are, just on the edge and unconscious, and next to you I am trying to find the remote without waking you or your shower curtained neighbor. Nowhere. "Ladies and Gentleman, my next guest needs no introduction. He has been a good friend of mine for (inaudible) years, and is a true humanitarian." OK, OK, I will add *All That Jazz* to the triptych. Memory is a beast, and some of us who lack imagination recast our past over the tableau of a film or a song. For years now, I recall the act of coring that apple bedside, picking up sparkling water off of Foothill on my ride to that place, crying in the parking lot, driving home open windowed to 6:00 am strip mall sprinklers so I could shave, take a shower and eat something before going to work in a Roy Scheideresque Fosse edit. It should be JB Lenoir or Roy Acuff or even The Rolling Stones that, when crawling through the speakers, call to mind you; instead, that song, because of that night when you tucked the god damn remote under your leg and left me with *Pippin*, it is that George Benson song that opens *All That Jazz*. You were probably as ambivalent about that song as I, but here it is overhead and it is getting to me again. "On Broadway," what kind of epitaph is that? You would laugh loud over that one last hilarious punch line we shared.

One dusk a year before those 2am eves in Upland. We had gone to your favorite Japanese restaurant where the proprietor recognized you. "Nice to see you" he said, to which you responded, as you always did, "Nice to be seen." Over the meal, we talked Bristol Sessions, hated on Alan Lomax, you pulled a Grandpa Jones CD on Bear Family out of a bag next to you, asked me if I knew his stuff. I recalled seeing him on *Hee Haw* when I was young to which you responded, "Aw shit dude, he cheapened himself on that, you have to go back." Nostalgia is for suckers, but that is no excuse not to stick your hands through the chest of the earth and dig.

Ernest Tubb died of emphysema in Nashville, 1982. Webb Pierce died of pancreatic cancer, Nashville, 1991. Banjo player, Grandpa Jones died of a stroke, Nashville 1998. John Harrelson, Upland, June 26, 2013.

CLAUDIA LENNEAR
TEW

THAT DWARF PEAR TREE you planted in the southwest corner of the backyard, I thought then was the perfect home for it. It grew up so slow and bared no fruit for six years. Here in the southwest, things take time. We braced you from the weight of your upper reach, tarps and smudge pots during those winterless heats. Meet one, and heat 2 and round three. There is that still life painted on the far wall, must be twenty or more yards from your window, that painting of that oak tree, with one last errant leaf, hanging on. Others here, to it, it does speak about perseverance & faith & hope & desperate cling. Your inimitable buoyant voice, on the darkest of days, laughing about how you just wish that that last god damn leaf would plant itself on the ground, that it has overstayed its season.

It it.

That that.

We are braced not by two by fours nor PVC piping dug into the ground next to us, built to hold up our sides that sway, but by artists and their works. Decades and decades of readingviewinglisteningseeing and rereadingreviewingrelisteningreseeing hundreds of thousands of pieces of art. Others may see their life flash before them, but I instead will hear and see every film and novel and newsprint smudge pass before me before I go, every shitty nickel ante kitty that I invested my time and dime in, every unexpected turn on the TV when I was expecting gristle, the surprise around the bend in a museum in Philly or Pomona. Your voice registering from the intake vent by the stove, feeding into my bedroom as I awake on some Sunday AM. I am listening, even when I am asleep. I go to bed knowing I won't make it through the director commentary, but it serves me and sends me as I imagine those old hardcovers of John Ford films served others in the early sixties.

Sweet exorcism, that voice that was always around you, ghostly in a sepia background, when it was finally called out from the wooden wheeled fence where it was appearing as an apparition in the dark, it becomes apparent why. That light too bright, that soul too deep, for one mic and some lime light. How can you sit with Claudia Lennear and, as a friend, not fall in love with her and champion her? Hers, a life of collaboration lifting others up, even now; if it isn't her students, then it is the members of her band. In an unassuming way she might mention David Bowie at her mom's place in Pomona in the '80s, or Allen Toussaint or her pal Chris Darrow that lives up the street. You are championing her because you know that she is a champ; a world of KOs behind her in worlds that she conquered with her winning smile and that endless love of hers for life. There are no regrets; there is only the past and the possibility of all of them futures before her. She has seen so much, but she won't dim the windshield with the dark of where she was before with Ike Turner. She won't mention the dead ends and the hard begins, she will ask about you, about "How you have been?," and about "How are your kids?," and about "How is your family?"

Some cling to the velvet curtain, the three nights on top in Tulsa or Tokyo, the high school yearbook, the prep squad, the post college European jaunt. She will mention in passing Mick Jagger, or Taj Mahal, or George Harrison. Those three don't mean a whole lot to me; they are not my holy trinity. From some session musician or fellow bandmate, these asides would be B-sides that I wouldn't flip but once out of curiosity. Over coffee at a local dive, we have breakfast for dinner, and we talk about Sharon Jones and Charles Bradley and Gram Parsons. Neither of us is the star struck type, so we fall in quick with a shorthand, to move along to all that there is to talk about tonight. When you meet Claudia Lennear, whose vocals dotted so many records that line your collection, you cannot help but see before you one who is selfless in this world of self-promotion. She doesn't mention in our twenty conversations Spooner Oldham, Jim Keltner or Ringo Starr. She mentions your children, and we talk about her daughter and we talk politics and art and of other things.

It matters not where we are planted. We, we are lucky as we can always choose to leave. Some of us leave every eve and you wouldn't even know it, but that is us unscrewing our feet from the compartment that holds batteries, that is us, into another world we do go. Lennear is listening closely in a world of broadcasters. In turn, I pay attention. Most people that you have met, and are going to meet, they are thinking only of cells and selves; things to collect and house, expressions of our meager body and mind's needs. We are trying, most of us, always, to serve higher purposes, and higher needs. Solo records and solitary settings to genuflect; personal trainers and underschooled psychologists we pay to swim through the worthless download stream of our beings. The act of speaking is passive, easy. The act of listening closely, that takes concentration and strength. Listen or look a little closer, for an artist as thoughtful and quiet as Lennear, for she doesn't need to turn a resume in to anyone. In fact, the job will be done before you even know it was starting.

SIMON JOYNER
FLASH FORWARD TO THE MOON

" **I** REMEMBER I SENT HIM my first cassette, asking if he would be interested in releasing it, and he wrote me back, replying that it looked like I had already released it myself." Simon is standing in my kitchen, leaning on the sink talking to Jarvis from Woods who has been flown to California to record Simon & me, laughing as he recounts from memory. The cassette Simon was talking about was entitled *Umbilical Chords*, and it was a professional cassette with a color J card, factory duped, wrapped in plastic. It was leagues from the handmade, recorded-over tapes I had been releasing. I remember listening to it quite a bit, trying to decide if it I liked it or hated it before I wrote the above back to him. I fell into this non middle ground indecision mostly under these kinds of lights. It would be music that I was being asked to release, sent to me by a stranger who dropped their cassette in the post to me blind. Listen closer, pay attention to the lyrics, microphone placement, and take in the way everything laid together all carpentered up. It is a complicated algorithm that begs for everything to be perfectly askew and unique enough to draw in my curiosity. Do you want to spend hours and hours dubbing this tape, does it mean that much to you? Investing time and money you don't really have on this strange ritual of yours? Am I doing the world a disservice if I don't at least plant this thing for the future in my tiny backyard?

I can easily recall that emotional ambivalence turning itself into a stalwart champion for some strangers I had never met. This weird wash of emotional vagueness was present when I first got a package of music from John Davis, and years later when an early Woods tape hit my PO Box. Catherine, do I like this, do I hate this, what do you think? She says "I don't know," religiously, which in all three of these cases sealed it for me. She remains so much more patient than me, and her calm shrug would push me in a direction. Make up your mind. Make a choice. I just had to verbalize that question out loud, out of body, so that I could then answer it.

You never want to meet your heroes, but if your peers become your heroes, well then, you are in rarefied air. What I could pen about Simon in closing this book, could easily be said in different ways, with specific concrete examples, of so many of the artists whose music I have put out over the years via this tiny cottage hobby shop that is Shrimper Records and Tapes. The laughter and love under the struggles and birth of all of them records. I mention this only as side two nears to a close as my publisher and pal of thirty years wrote me a missive just this afternoon. It was regarding the completed manuscript that I had turned into him and he in turn sent back the final corrected proof of today. "That last chapter, which is titled 'Simon Joyner,' cannot simply be the acknowledgements." It doesn't make sense I practically hear his shoulders in the air through the screen trying to explain. I know he is right; just as he was right about the one chapter that didn't sit well with him which was the one chapter that I couldn't retrain to convey what I meant after days of playing with the dead thing. He pushed gently into the weakened tissue, leaving the whole of the rest of the body of the thing unscathed. How could he know? I think back to what this chapter could then be about. The cursor wasn't hungry, wasn't staring back impatiently at me. It was just blinking at me, an "I'm here," take your time kind of maternal blink waiting for this one last thing that you thought you needn't tell.

You little underdog, you scrappy little stray. It took you five years to get an AA at a junior college, working graveyard at a gas station then. No one taught you how to do anything. You were ill-prepared for moving out at 18, for getting married at 23, for having a kid at 25. No one taught you how to do those things. No one showed you how to raise a family. And all them lesser things, no one gave you the manual on how to run a record label. No one taught you and your pals how to lay out a zine or run an access cable TV show or DJ on college radio or be some kind of manager or general manager of a couple of record stores. It was not one, it was all of them. It was reverse Ayn Rand. It was all collective. All that scraping and the pulling and anteing up between so many of us; shoving a piano into Bob Durkee's van so we could get it to the club for the diva from New Zealand, booking shows in laundromats, recording sessions in body shops after hours. The perverted hippy dream turned punk rock of no machine and no contract and no ownership of nothing.

A record label is a trap, a trap as bad as a publicist or a manager or a need to fill some cavernous market with sausage. I reminded myself religiously not to become part of that world. I had seen so many turn into exactly what they railed against. Some secret they knew like a Michael Jackson Thillerbot revealing the monster he is back when no one could believe such things. It is the minor steps. It is the slow descent. It is 7:49 in the PM on Tuesday May the 14th and you are barely flying, always at risk of crashing. The Ontario, California tarmac is so close it is almost at our feet and only now is it coming to me. These imagined tapes already existed—they were those you were entrusted to release and care for by strangers and family and friends. They were your life then, and now they are a slight history for some teen to fetishize. Breadcrumbs, detours, like the ones you are unaware you are slipping into deep into night, pulled away from a novel, staring at the words, not reading a damn thing. Daydreaming about Anne-Marie Miéville. What might a painting by her look like? Taste like? Oils and vinegars and weeds. What would she do next with next to nothing?

PLAY-PAUSE-FORWARD-REWIND

BY ALLEN CALLACI

MY BROTHER ONCE told me that one of the things he admired most about the cassette format was how unyielding it was. If you felt you were moments away of unlocking the elusive secret to the universe after listening to Dylan's "It's Alright, Ma (I'm Only Bleeding)" but needed another quick listen to confirm this you would find yourself caught in a frustrating tug-of-war between the track that proceeded it, "Gates of Eden", and the track that followed it "It's All Over Now Baby Blue." Unlike vinyl where one could just plop the needle back down on the track they wished to re-hear, or a CD where one could instantly skip back to their favorite track or today's technologically advanced devices where one can instantly call a track back up, the cassette required a Sisyphean commitment of constant rewind, fast forward and rewind in order to replay that certain song. There has never been another musical format that requires so much physical engagement on behalf of the listener.

Listening to a cassette is an exercise in frustration and reward.

And frustration and reward are the pillars upon which great art is balanced on.

There is something intrinsically and tragically human about cassettes. It does not matter how meticulously one pampers a cassette their lifespan can never be accurately predicted –the highest quality/high bias cassette tapes played in the most expensive cassette decks are just as likely to have their fragile innards mangled beyond recognition as a low resolution cassette lodged in the dusty mouth of a cassette player of a 1983 Pinto. With each year that passes the cassette becomes more and more of a loud, defiant spit into the eye of the current state of ageless and graceless digital perfection and instant gratification.

I have no argument to make with the tired cliché that music is the soundtrack to our lives. Inside each song lies a high-powered time machine with the ability to instantly transport the listener to a certain time and place. The format of the cassette doubles down on this sentiment with brutal precision. It can conjure up memories of driving past The Boot Barn, and Western Connection and the fake old western themed streets of downtown San Dimas in 1993 with X's *More Fun in the New World* ironically spinning and spurning out of the back speakers of a used Subaru, or carrying a Panasonic rx 4830 boom box loaded up with a handful of fresh copper top batteries and cassette copies of Iron Maiden *Killers* and Jesus and Mary Chain *Darklands* through the sands for a late 80's Newport Beach bonfire, or the rite of passage of taping over the tabs of Dokken's *Tooth and Nail* and recording Nick Cave's *Henry's Dream* over it to accommodate ever evolving musical tastes.

This collection refutes this notion that there could ever be such thing as an instant and permanent musical makeover. This collection presents the cassette as a metaphor for human existence. We might try to record over and extinguish pieces of our past but they can never be fully exorcised. Despite our best efforts they will always be there, lingering and bleeding through in the background for a focused ear to pick up on. This collection conjures up times and places that are achingly personal and bends them towards the universal. And like a beloved, well-worn cassette in a cracked plastic case the pages you hold before you call for the endless return of your fingertips to the play-pause-forward- and rewind buttons.

ACKNOWLEDGMENTS

T HERE WAS ALWAYS MUSIC around both of the houses I was raised in. There was a piano, a guitar, 8-tracks, records, it was all in the air that my parents populated the house with. My older sister and older brother, they would pull fresh kills into the house that would become part of our musical language. Do you know how dark this Simon & Garfunkel song "Richard Cory" is, one of them would ask an eight-year-old. What is a "Grapevine," "Undercover Angel," why not "Rock The Boat" and tip the boat over? Questions that in time would be answered, for the most part, disappointingly. No artist resides in a vacuum. Even if the radio is off, the movie theater is closed and their library is nothing more than a dusty remnant with an awful curator of tomes. Mishear something from a friend, grab an idea from the way a passerby stumbles off the curb, the blood on a storefront window—any of these things may be the string that leads and makes something out of itself.

There are the thousands upon thousands of songs and records and artists that have formed and informed me. From the abstract, to the living and breathing that shared shitty bills or shitty rental cars or shittier watering holes or your beautiful cassettes, CDs, LPs or 7″ releases with me in some way or another. This book is in essence an autobiography. My sister told me that before it was written. My brother and I have told our life story in a language that at many times is even lost to us, lost on us, in a state of unawares until sometimes decades later when we are dusting off a song one or the other of us has found the key of truth it was based on. Creating comics when I was eight with him, writing poems at nine with my sister and using this mediocre talent to later collaborate on a cable access TV shows weekly in our late teens shepherded by Allen; then a zine, a band, a record label, a ten-year-running radio show, booker of hundreds of shows dotting the greater Inland Empire stretch, a job at a record store. Surely, minor accomplishments, all of them, but none done alone. Franklin Bruno getting a gig booked and letting me flesh out a couple of the bands on the bill, Robert Vodicka whose work at New Alliance Records allowed me to pester him about how to get records made. John Golden, not laughing at a twenty-year-old bringing bags of cassettes in to be sequenced, mastered, and cut to wax. Graveyard shifts at a gas station to put myself through Chaffey College? OK, that was one of the few things that was not done with the help of anyone else and I barely remember doing any of it. No fireworks, just some quiet conspiring for a lifetime between two or more of us.

To raise my boys with my wife of over twenty-five years, to have lived those years and not have to walk home with a ghostwritten laundry list of regret to any of the four-way stop signs when I pause, thank you Catherine. Dozens of times you allowed me to turn down cheap quicks, to not once raise a flag about money and time into something when we had so many other things before us. For reminding me that none of it matters when in times of treachery. Thank you to my extended family, but firstly to my brother and sister who gave me language and possibilities and my folks for not crushing me. To the three kids that Catherine and I helped raise, Rael, Henry and Harmonie. To the thousands of people that over thirty years, I had the luck of collaborating with in one way or another musically. Sure, the world is made up of miscreants and idiots, but dig harder and be diligent about your discards. It isn't a book, or a song, but your love and friendship at day's end. Lucy Beloian, Bill Chen, Susan Brooks, Robert Vodicka, John Golden, Gary Held, Bob Durkee, Mark Givens, Franklin Bruno & Nothing Painted Blue, Simon Joyner, Lou Barlow, Amps For Christ, WCKR SPGT, Junket, Goosewind, Daniel Brodo, Joel Connell, Chris Jones, Aaron Alcala, Ira Kaplan, James

McNew, Yo La Tengo, Chris Knox, Bill Callahan, Tim Adams, Chris Toovey, Margaret Aichele, Nathan Wilson, Chuck Oken Jr., John Davis, The Ah Club, Soul Junk, Joy, Tres Oui, Jeremy Earl, Jarvis Tavierne, Kevin Morby, Buzzsaw, Jive, Wild Wild Bacuum Car, John Harrelson, John Darnielle, Anthems of Carnea, Amy Maloof, Kristi Engle, Diskothi-Q, God Is My Co-Pilot, Paul K, Halo, The Secret Stars, Scott Feemster, Pie, Big Breakfast, Bingo Trappers, Herman Dune, Emil Hagstrom, Near Castlegar, Good Horsey, Larry Cash Jr, The Azusa Plane, Linda Smith, Patch, The Irving Klaw Trio, Furniture Huschle, Montessouri, Keslo, Paul & Laura, Fishstick, Charlie Parker, Mote, The Goblins, Jad Fair & Jason Willet, The Primordial Undermind, Jim Shepard, Charles Cicerella, The Aum Rifle, Adam Lipman, John Thill, Whitman, Woods, The Babies, Donovan Quinn, The Debts, The Uncalled For, Sebadoh, Will Simmons, The Sloppy Heads, Pork Queen, Creeper Lagoon, Post Life and the myriad of artists who have allowed me to release music by them over the years; all of them, without a contract, all of them on a handshake and faith. I have blathered on and on, and I can see through the shell's window that there isn't much tape left, just a few more seconds before the tail tightens around the supply reel and automatically clicks the play to an end. Black magnetic to red lead and then that final snap that ends side two.

ABOUT THE AUTHOR

DENNIS CALLACI WAS BORN in Corona, California and has bounced around Southern California his entire life. He runs the record label Shrimper, noted for bringing forth the earliest recordings from Amps For Christ, Woods, Franklin Bruno, Lou Barlow's Sentridoh, The Mountain Goats, Dump, Kevin Morby, The Secret Stars, and a few hundred other releases over the course of the last thirty years. He is also in the band Refrigerator who have released twelve records over those thirty years, as well as solo records by Callaci & collaborations with John Davis, The Debts, and Simon Joyner. A former KSPC DJ, booker of shows around Southern California, and GM of two record stores of note, music has eaten up the majority of his life.

CPSIA information can be obtained
at www.ICGtesting.com
Printed in the USA
FSHW020850300120
66489FS